TALES OF THE
IRISH
HEDGEROWS

TONY LOCKE

The History Press

To our beautiful and talented grandchildren,
Jake, Calum, Bronwyn and Michael.

This book is also dedicated to my wife and soul mate, Gaynor.
With love and appreciation for all her support over the years.

First published 2017
This paperback edition published 2020

The History Press
97 St George's Place
Cheltenham,
Gloucestershire,
GL50 3QB

www.thehistorypress.co.uk

British Library Cataloguing in Publication Data.
A catalogue record for this book is available from the British Library.

ISBN 978 0 7509 9570 2
Typesetting and origination by The History Press
Printed and bound in Great Britain by TJ Books Limited, Padstow

CONTENTS

ACKNOWLEDGEMENTS

THIS BOOK WOULD NOT have been possible without the support and encouragement of my wife, Gaynor. My words cannot express my gratitude for the amount of time she gave to proofreading and offering her advice and guidance.

I also acknowledge all those storytellers past and present, for a story does not become a story until it is shared and in the sharing it makes the journey a lot shorter.

INTRODUCTION

THE FLORA AND FAUNA of the Irish hedgerow have played a major part in the shaping of the Irish countryside. The hedgerow is a rich and diverse habitat that supports a wide range of plants and animals. They not only depend upon each other for their existence but also upon their human neighbours. It is this relationship that has influenced the history, landscape, and aesthetic beauty of Ireland and it continues to contribute to the life of the Irish people.

How important is folklore in contemporary Irish society? Does it have any place in modern thinking and can we recapture the mystery and sense of wonder that appears to be at odds with the modern, fast-moving Ireland of today? We have as a nation evolved to a point where folklore is looked upon by many as superstition, a belief in things that have no relevance to life today. We humans have always had a close relationship with things that exist just beyond our scope of vision, those things that live in the realms of make-believe and yet provide both a moral compass and a conscience. Superstition and myth are bedfellows of Irish folklore and it is these twin aspects of the Irish psyche that make up our natural and cultural heritage.

A superstition is a belief or a practice that is not based on facts or events that can be proven. Yet it is part of who and what we are and in many ways it makes us human. Superstition is part of our imagination; without it, we would never have evolved in the way we have. Without imagination, we would simply accept things at face value; we would not question what we see or don't see, hear or don't hear. We need to have a balance between superstition and rationality in order to evolve on an intellectual level. Folklore encompasses superstition — various types of flora and fauna, for example, are considered either as omens of good luck or bad luck and the stories associated with them can be quite diverse and are usually integrated with the natural features of the landscape. A study of our folklore and superstition can reveal aspects of the ever-evolving nature, culture and people of Ireland. Folklore is constantly changing to fit in with new ways of thinking and is also being added to by the influx of different cultural traditions. As people repeat the stories told to them, they may add or embellish them and in some ways stories become richer for it.

Belief in these old superstitions is no longer as strong as it was in the days before modern science, but they nonetheless continue to be part of the richness and uniqueness of Irish culture. Some of the traditions of Irish folklore are in danger of being forgotten altogether — from belief in magical cures and holy wells to the superstitions concerning unlucky omens and fairy trees. While these beliefs may seem strange and out-dated to outsiders, I believe they give richness and meaning to life and I hope they will continue to do so in the future.

We live in a time where almost anything we want to know is easy for us to find out. We turn on the television and get the local weather or do a search on the internet and most of the time come up with whatever information we need. The past generations did not have this available to them; they learned by observing their world and listening to the elders of their communities. As modern children become more and more detached from the natural world around them, they may begin to lose interest in the wonders of nature and the folklore and superstitions of their ancestors. They who manage to retain an interest appear to get little or no support from the educational system. However, in order to equip the future generations in ways to deal with the ever-increasing environmental problems with which this world is faced, a knowledge of the natural world is vital.

Folklore is in constant flux; it is made up of the stories of the community who in the past were mostly illiterate. They were dependent upon hearing, seeing, imitating and remembering. Folklore contains the accumulated knowledge passed down by those who have gone before, the 'tradition bearers'. As we say in Irish, '*ó ghlúin go glúin*' (from knee to knee). However, the folklore of a people is not only the stories that are told; it also includes the myths, legends, and superstitions, herbal remedies and recipes.

The Importance of the Irish Hedgerow

Both flora and fauna co-exist in an intricate network of mainly indigenous trees, shrubs and flowers, which are a unique part of our landscape. Ireland was once a heavily wooded country; however, over time most of our woodland has disappeared as the demand for timber from various sources increased. Regretfully, hedgerows are now suffering the same fate. Small farms and fields are amalgamated to make more manageable and financially efficient businesses. This has resulted in the eradication of hedgerows and boundaries, leading to both a loss of habitat and folklore, as Ireland is defined by its place names and landmarks, which are dictated by the landscape.

The growth of population and the associated need for housing, services, and transportation networks has added to this loss of hedgerows. However, poor hedgerow management is also a reason for their decline, as they need to be properly maintained using traditional techniques, such as hedgelaying, to ensure their health, vitality and proper functioning. Hedgelaying is the traditional way a hedgerow was maintained as it creates a thick, impenetrable barrier that keeps livestock contained while revitalising the hedge. This process can actually extend the lifespan of most hedgerows indefinitely and is aesthetically pleasing. Unfortunately this type of management is labour intensive and therefore it comes with associated cost; it is more cost effective to use a tractor fitted with a flail to cut back hedgerows – but the devastation this causes to both the hedgerow and the wildlife is heart-breaking to see.

The importance of the hedgerow in Ireland cannot be overstated. They are in many ways nature's highway, a way for small mammals, insects, and butterflies to travel from one area to another. The Irish hedgerow provides a wildlife corridor, which affords animals shelter from the elements, safety from predators and a food supply. Within the hedgerow, you will find that many different species have created a home for themselves. Animals and birds depend upon the hedgerows and we in turn depend upon them. The loss of hedgerows is having a devastating effect upon this biodiversity as the habitat and ecosystem that supports our wildlife is changing at such a rate it seems impossible for a number of species to adapt.

When I was a young boy, I often went out picking blackberries, wild strawberries and sloe berries with other members of my family (a practice I continue to this day). This not only gave us the benefit of the fruit, which was then used in various jams, pies and tarts, but also enabled us to see if there were any gaps in the hedges where livestock could escape (which we would then report back to the elders), nesting birds and other wildlife. Having returned home with the 'fruits of our labours', we would then help in the preparation of the treats to come. We would be regaled with tales and stories about the things that we had seen and a world that no longer exists except within the imagination of a young child. Within the pages of this book, I will attempt to take you, the reader, on a journey through the Irish hedgerow, to a time when life was just that little bit simpler.

THE ELDER

(*Trom*)

Trí comartha láthraig mallachtan: tromm, tradna, nenaid.
(Three tokens of a cursed site: elder, a corncrake, nettles.)

According to this old Irish saying, there are three signs of a cursed or barren place: the elder, the nettle and the lonesome calling corncrake. This has some basis in truth, as the elder is a very early coloniser of bare land; the seed of this pioneer species can be spread through droppings from passing birds.

The elder is considered to have a *crostáil* (a bad temper or mischief) in it and it was believed that if someone were struck with an elder branch, after their death their hand would grow out of their grave. Because of its association with witches, elder is said to be hostile to children, especially infants. It is considered dangerous and foolhardy, therefore, to make a cradle out of elder as it could cause the child to sicken and be stolen away by the fairies. It is also said to be wrong to strike a child or animal with a piece of elder, as it would cause them to stop growing from that day onwards. The leaves have a scent that is slightly narcotic and there is an old legend that warns against sleeping under the elder because you may not wake up.

Many Christians believe that elder is the tree from which Judas Iscariot hanged himself after betraying Jesus. It is also said that the cross upon which Christ was crucified was made from elder wood. In Ireland it was believed that the elder tree refused to shelter Christ but the ivy did so. From that time on, the elder was the last tree to come into leaf each spring, while the ivy is evergreen.

The elder has been held in high esteem throughout our history as a medicinal plant and has even earned the name 'the medicine chest of the country folk'. Parts of the elder are used to treat everything from burns to the common cold and it has been suggested that extract of elderberry may be effective in the treatment of the bird flu virus. Today extracts of elder are used in skin cleansers and another legend suggests that if a young girl washes her face in the morning dew of the elderflower she will remain young-looking. This may also be because the berries contain dyes that were used to darken grey hair.

The elder, in common with the hawthorn and the rowan, has strong associations with the fairy folk and is a tree of protection. It is considered very lucky if you have one growing near your house. Traditionally a rowan would be grown at the front of the house, while the elder's place would be at the back door, keeping evil influences from entering your home. The aroma exuded by the elder's leaves has long been known to repel flies, so this folklore may have been borne out of the need to keep such insects, and the diseases that they carried, away from the kitchen and food. Bunches of leaves were hung by doorways, in livestock barns, and attached to horses' harnesses for the same reason.

Elder was traditionally planted around dairies as it was thought to be efficacious in keeping the milk from 'turning'. Cheese cloths and other linen involved in dairying were hung out to dry on elder trees, and the smell they absorbed from the leaves may have contributed to hygiene in the dairy.

Elder trees were also traditionally planted by bake houses as protection from the Devil (presumably attracted by all those hellishly hot ovens within!) and loaves and cakes were put out to cool under the elders. Any foods left out overnight under an elder, however, were considered a gift to the fairies.

It is sometimes called the 'hollow tree' because the spongy tissue within its smaller branches can be easily removed, thus providing hollow tubes, and many felt that this hollow offered a door into the fairy kingdom.

The elder tree was also said to have the power of walking in the twilight and peering into a child's window when the child was alone.

The flowers make a delicious cordial or wine, while the elderberries are a very good source of vitamin C and also make wonderful jelly and wines – but don't forget to leave some for the birds.

THE WILD CHERRY

THE WILD CHERRY IS also known as the bird cherry as the fruit is used as a food source by a large variety of birds. You have to be quick if you want to beat the birds to the abundant crop that results from a good spring and summer, and the cherries are often picked when they are still a yellowish-red colour, before they ripen to deep reddish purple. They can be used in pies, wine, liquors and even a dessert soup.

Wild cherries were used to flavour alcoholic drinks such as whisky or gin, and cherry brandy can easily be made by filling a bottle with wild cherries, adding sugar and brandy and leaving for a few months. The bark was used to make fabric dyes, ranging in colour from cream to tan, while a reddish-purple colour was derived from the roots.

The resin that leaks from the trunk was formerly used by children as chewing gum. It is recorded as a treatment for coughs, and when it was dissolved in wine, it was used to treat gallstones and kidney stones.

Wild cherry leaves are generally regarded as safe when used in recommended doses. However, since they contain small amounts of cyanide, they should not be taken in anything other than very small doses. They should never be taken by young children, pregnant women or those who have liver or kidney problems. There has been some evidence suggesting that wild cherry may interact with various medications, so I would think very carefully before taking it.

THE BLACKTHORN

(*Draighean*)

ALSO KNOWN AS MOTHER of the woods, dark mother of the woods, pear hawthorn, wishing thorn and spiny plum and of course the sloe, the blackthorn is depicted in many fairy tales throughout Europe as a tree of ill omen. Called *straif* in Ogham, this tree has the most sinister reputation in Celtic tree lore. The English word 'strife' is said to derive from this Celtic word.

The tree is linked with warfare, wounding and death. The Irish cudgel – called a *bata* or *shillelagh* – is usually made from blackthorn, although it can be made from oak, ash or holly. This is a hard, strong, plentiful wood that also has a very convenient knob that is formed from the root of the shrub. Its bark is especially tough and the wood was cured by burying it in a dung heap or smearing it with butter then placing it up the chimney for up to a month. (Blackthorn wood is also the traditional wood for walking sticks, due to its durability and rich colour when polished.)

The blackthorn is often associated with darkness, winter, and the waning or dark moon; a particularly cold spring is referred to as 'a Blackthorn winter'. It is a sacred tree to the Dark, or Crone, aspect of the Triple Goddess, and is known as 'the increaser and keeper of dark secrets'. It is associated with the Cailleach – the Crone of Death, and the Irish Morrigan. Winter begins when the Cailleach (also the goddess of winter) strikes the ground with her blackthorn staff.

The devil was said to prick the fingers of his followers with blackthorn to seal their pact. It is considered the opposite of the benign hawthorn (which is also known as whitethorn), with which it so frequently grows. The blackthorn's spines are extremely hard and can cause a great deal of bleeding; the wound inflicted by them will often turn septic. They were frequently used as pins by English witches and became known as the 'pin of slumber'. The shrub was denounced as a witch's tool by the Church and therefore the wood of the blackthorn was used for the pyres of witches and heretics. They were also maliciously placed under horses' saddles, causing the horses to throw their riders when the spines pieced the horses' flesh, causing injury or death to the unfortunate riders.

For all its deadly associations, blackthorn is also associated with the concept of the cycle of life and death and protection, and has a number of practical physical uses. Blackthorn often topped the maypole entwined with hawthorn while at New Year celebrants made blackthorn crowns, which they burned in the New Year's fire. The ashes were used to fertilise the fields. Where blackthorn grows near its sister plant the hawthorn, the site is especially magical.

The blackthorn is also seen as a protective tree and representative of the endless cycle of life and death. The flowers appear before the leaves in the spring, heralding the start of that season and providing blossom whilst there is still snow on the ground and everything else still seems dead from its winter sleep. Its dense branches protect the year's new chicks from predation and in their adulthood provide them with food when many other species of plant have lost their berries. Along with the hawthorn, it has long been favoured by farmers as a hedging shrub.

The blossom was used in ancient fertility rites as well as being hung in the bedchamber of a bride on her wedding night. It is a thicket of these trees that protects sleeping beauty in her castle, and witches in northern England would carve the symbol for thorn on a blackthorn staff for protection.

The tree itself is said to be protected by the fairy folk. It is considered a fairy tree and is protected by the *lunantishee*, a type of fairy that inhabits it. They will not allow a mortal to cut blackthorn on 11 May or 11 November, the original dates of Bealtaine and Samhain before the calendar was changed. Great misfortune will befall anyone who ignores this. The *lunantishee* may also be the *leannán sidhe* or fairy lover.

Hawthorne flowers are a diuretic and depurative (or blood purifier), useful as a spring cleansing tonic and for skin conditions such as acne. The bark is used as an astringent and to treat fever and is also gathered in the spring. The leaves are astringent and diuretic, while the unripe fruit is used to treat acne. There is mention of combining the leaves, bark, fruits and flowers together for certain traditional cures; presumably some of these would be in dried form. The ripe fruit is traditionally gathered after the first frost, which sweetens the taste. They are used to prepare sloe gin, or as a winter fruit to add to pies and jams or to brew wine.

The Lunantishee *or* Leannán Sidhe

As mentioned previously, the blackthorn is protected by a group of fairy folk, known in Irish folklore as the *Lunantishee* or *Leannán Sidhe*. They will not take kindly to anyone who attempts to cut down or even harm any part of the blackthorn and woe betides anyone who ignores this advice.

Known throughout the Celtic world, the name *Leannán Sidhe* means 'Fairy of Inspiration' or 'Love Fairy'. It is an extremely dangerous dark and evil creature, often depicted as a vampire-like spirit that sucks the life-force from its victims. In Irish folklore, the *Leannán Sidhe* is a muse of poetry or music and it is said that those that devote themselves to it will live a short but glorious life. It has even been described as giving the gift of creativity in exchange for the artist's life. However, to be fair, it may be the destructive nature of the artist that has given rise to the description of the *Leannán Sidhe* as evil and dangerous. Musicians, artists, writers and poets often tend to burn the candle at both ends; they burn brightly but can expire quickly. The depth of depression they sink to when the *Leannán Sidhe* leaves them usually results in great heartbreak or sorrow. This is the price demanded for the gift of inspiration.

Whatever you think of the *Leannán Sidhe*, whether you regard it as something to be feared or something to be embraced, once captured you live only in order to please. You will be ensnared within the arms of a dominatrix – the more you suffer, the more you will crave; the more you feed off them the more you will hunger and that hunger will never be satisfied. You will sacrifice everything and will be consumed by your own passion.

It has been suggested that the blackthorn was used by the ancient Gaelic poets as a symbol of female beauty; because of its white/pale flowers and black bark, it was said to reflect the fair skin and jet black hair of the Irish maiden. The *Leannán Sidhe*, on the other hand, has been described as a skinny, ugly, old hairless man with pointed ears, long sharp teeth, scrawny long arms and talon-like fingers. They are said to travel in groups that live in the branches of the blackthorn tree. They hate humans with a passion and will go to great lengths to avenge themselves upon any who dare to harm their beloved blackthorn.

Whether you see the *Lunantishee* or *Leannán Sidhe* as a pale-skinned beauty or an ugly old man, my advice to you would be to leave the blackthorn where it is and just keep walking by. It would not be wise to antagonise the fairy folk.

THE HAWTHORN

(Sceach Gheal)

THE HAWTHORN IS KNOWN by a variety of different names:
the May tree, the Bealtaine tree, the May blossom, the whitethorn,
the quick, etc. In Irish it is *Sceach Geal*, but we also know it as the
Fairy Tree for it is said to guard the entrance to the fairy realm
and it is still considered bad luck to harm one. You may, however,
collect sprigs of flowers during the month of May to place in and
around the home to banish evil spirits or misfortune (but always
ask the guardians of the tree first).

There are many superstitions surrounding the hawthorn and here are just a few of them:

If a calf is born prematurely, hanging its afterbirth on a hawthorn tree was said to magically protect it and give it quick growth (one of the other names given to the hawthorn is 'quickset' as it will take very easily as a cutting). This could be magic by association.

The hawthorn has long been associated with fertility and at Bealtaine (1 May) young women would take a sprig of blossom and keep it close as a way of attracting a husband. On the morning of Bealtaine (dawn), men and women would bathe in the morning dew of the hawthorn blossom to increase wealth, health, luck, good fortune, and beauty. Women would become more beautiful and men, by washing their hands in the dew, would become skilled craftsmen. Today it is still practised and it is one of the woods used in the hand-fastening ritual, as it will ensure a lasting relationship.

The hawthorn is also known as a tree of protection and for this reason it will often be found growing near a house. It will offer protection from storms and lightning.

On Bealtaine it is the custom to hang strips of cloth or ribbons on a hawthorn (especially if it grows near a well) in order to make a wish (the wishing tree of legend). This is also done to ask for Brigid's blessing on the cloth, which will then be used in healing (I hang crepe bandages on ours). It is also the custom to hang strips of coloured cloth from the branches: blue for health, red or pink for love, green or gold for prosperity, etc. These will then be used as bindings in the hand fastening.

You may use discarded pieces of wood in order to make wands or ritual tools but NEVER cut the wood from the tree. If you look in winter you will ALWAYS find pieces of windblown wood.

Hawthorn has an immense amount of folklore attached to it in Ireland. The young leaves and flower buds were eaten in spring salads and commonly referred to as bread and cheese and the blossom and berries were made into wines and jellies. Decoctions of the flowers and leaves were used medicinally to stabilise blood pressure. The infusion has been shown to be valuable in improving the heartbeat rate and strength, especially in heart failure, and in balancing the blood pressure; it also helps with irregular heartbeats and improves the peripheral circulation, helping with conditions such as Reynaud's and with poor memory since it improves blood circulation to the brain.

The bioflavonoids relax and dilate the arteries and blood vessels, thereby relieving angina. The bioflavonoids and proanthocyanins are also valuable antioxidants, which help repair and prevent tissue damage, especially in the blood vessels. Hawthorn also helps to relieve anxiety and is traditionally thought to mend broken hearts, both emotionally and physically.

The berries are gathered in the autumn and have similar medicinal properties – they can be used fresh or dried in a decoction or infused in brandy to make a heart tonic for the winter months. For culinary use, the berries are traditionally gathered after the first frost, which converts some of the starches to sugars and makes the berries more palatable. Berries are used as an ingredient in hedgerow wine, or to make haw jelly as an accompaniment to wild game. The berries can also be mashed, removing the skin and seeds, and used to make a fruit leather as a way of preserving them.

Thomas the Rhymer, the famous thirteenth-century Scottish mystic and poet, once met the Fairy Queen by a hawthorn bush from which a cuckoo was calling. She led him into the Fairy Underworld for a brief sojourn, but upon re-emerging into the world of mortals he found he had been absent for seven years. Themes of people being waylaid by the fairy folk to places where time passes differently are common in Celtic mythology, and the hawthorn was one of the most likely trees to be inhabited or protected by the Gentry. In Ireland most of the isolated trees, or so-called 'lone bushes', found in the landscape and said to be inhabited by fairies were hawthorn trees. Such trees could not be cut down or damaged in any way without incurring the often fatal wrath of their supernatural guardians. The Fairy Queen by her hawthorn can also be seen as a representation of an earlier pre-Christian archetype, reminding us of goddess-centred worship, practised by priestesses in sacred groves of hawthorn, planted in the round. The site of Westminster Abbey was once called Thorney Island after the sacred stand of thorn trees there.

Hawthorn is at its most prominent in the landscape when it blossoms during the month of May and probably the most popular of its many vernacular names is the May-tree. As such, it is the only plant that is named after the month in which it blooms. It has many associations with May Day festivities. Though the tree now flowers around the middle of the month, it flowered much nearer the beginning of the month, before the introduction of the Gregorian calendar in 1752.

The blossoms were used for garlands and large leafy branches were cut, set in the ground outside houses as so-called May bushes and decorated with local wildflowers. Using the blossoms for decorations outside was allowed, but there was a very strong taboo against bringing hawthorn into the house. In the early 1980s, the Folklore Society's survey of 'unlucky' plants revealed that 23 per cent of the items referred to hawthorn, more than twice as many instances as the second most unlucky plant, lilac. Across Ireland there was the belief that bringing hawthorn blossom into the house would be followed by illness and death, and there were many instances of hapless children being scolded by adults for innocently decorating the home. Mediaeval country folk also asserted that the smell of hawthorn blossom was just like the smell of death. Botanists later discovered that the chemical trimethylamine present in hawthorn blossom is one of the first chemicals formed in decaying animal tissue. In the past, when corpses would have been kept in the house for several days prior to burial, people would have been very familiar with the smell of death, so it is hardly surprising that hawthorn blossom was so unwelcome in the house.

It has also been suggested that some of the hawthorn (*Crataegus monogyna*) folklore may have originated for the related woodland hawthorn (*Crataegus laevigata*), which may well have been more common during the early Middle Ages, when a lot of plant folklore was evolving. Woodland hawthorn blossom gives off much more of an unpleasant scent of death soon after it is cut, and it also blooms slightly earlier than hawthorn, so that its blossoms would have been more reliably available for Bealtaine celebrations. It was normal to decorate a hawthorn at this time with flowers, ribbons and bright scraps of cloth and sometimes candles or rushlights were attached to the tree and lit on the eve of Bealtaine. In some areas of Ireland, small gifts of food and drink would be left under the tree for the fairies.

The strong, close-grained wood was used for carving and for making tool handles and other small household items. Probably its greatest practical use to people has been as hedging.

In common with other 'unlucky' trees, it was widely believed that whitethorn was the tree upon which Christ was crucified, and Christ's thorns were also supposed to have been made of whitethorn.

In Ireland it was believed that if one of your neighbours used a whitethorn (hawthorn) stick to herd cattle then he was up to no good. An old Irish custom was that the first milk of a newly calved cow should be taken and poured under a fairy tree as a tribute to the fairies. It was also planted around the house and sheds to keep away witches.

THE WILLOW

MOST WILLOW SPECIES GROW and thrive close to water or in damp places and this theme is reflected in the legends and magic associated with these trees. The moon too recurs as a theme, the movement of water being intimately bound up with and affected by the moon. For example, Hecate, the powerful Greek goddess of the moon and of willow, also taught sorcery and witchcraft and was 'a mighty and formidable divinity of the Underworld'. Helice was also associated with water and her priestesses used willow in their water magic and witchcraft. The willow muse, called Heliconian after Helice, was sacred to poets and the Greek poet Orpheus carried willow branches on his adventures in the Underworld. He was also given a lyre by Apollo and it is interesting to note that the sound boxes of harps used to be carved from solid willow wood.

Willow was often the tree most sought by the village wise-woman, since it has so many medicinal properties, and eventually the willow's healing and religious qualities became one and the tree came to be called the 'witch's tree'. The willow is also associated with the fey. The wind in the willows is the whisperings of a fairy in the ear of a poet. It is also said that willow trees can uproot themselves and stalk travellers at night, muttering at them.

Country folk have been familiar with the healing properties of willow for a long time. They made an infusion from the bitter bark as a remedy for colds and fevers and to treat inflammatory conditions such as rheumatism. Young willow twigs were also chewed to relieve pain. In the early nineteenth century, modern science isolated the active ingredient responsible, salicylic acid, which was also found in the meadowsweet plant. From this the world's first synthetic drug, acetylasylic acid, was developed and marketed as aspirin, named after the old botanical name for meadowsweet, *Spirea ulmaria*.

The willow is linked to grief and in the sixteenth and seventeenth centuries jilted lovers would wear wreaths of willow and many unrequited-love poems were written that made reference to the willow.

In Irish folklore it couldn't be more different as here it was called *sail ghlann grin* or the 'bright cheerful sallow'. Here it is considered lucky to take a sally rod with you on a journey and a sally rod was placed around a milk churn to ensure good butter. It was believed that the charcoal left behind after burning willow could be crushed and spread on the back of an animal as a way of increasing fertility and even restoring hair.

The willow, because of its link with water, milk and cattle, is particularly associated with the river goddess Bóinn. Bóinn was depicted as a great cow and the milk that flowed from her udders was said to form the waters of the Boyne.

It is estimated that the willow in Ireland provides support in the form of habitation and food for 266 different insect species. The willow is associated with enchantment, wishing, romantic love, healing, protection, fertility, death, femininity, divination, friendship, joy, love and peace. Placed in homes, willow branches protect against evil and malign sorcery. Carried, willow wood will give bravery, dexterity and help one overcome the fear of death. If you knock on a willow tree (knock on wood), this will avert evil. A willow tree growing near a home will protect it from danger. Willow is a good tree to plant around cemeteries and also for lining burial graves due to its symbolism of death and protection.

Willows can be used in rituals for intuition, knowledge, gentle nurturing, and will elucidate the feminine qualities of both men and women. If a person needs to get something off their chest or to share a secret, if they confess to a willow, their secret will be trapped. Wishes are also granted by a willow tree, if they are asked for in the correct manner. Willow leaves, bark and wood add energy to healing magic and burning a mix of willow bark and sandalwood during the waning moon can help to conjure spirits. Uses of willow in love talismans included wearing a sprig of willow around the wrist or using the leaves to make an infusion/tea.

THE ASH

(*Fuinseóg*)

THE FASCINATION OF THE ash tree traces its roots to the ancient times. The Druids believed that ash had the ability to direct and blend the masculine and feminine energy. Some Druids use a branch of the ash to make their staff. The staff then acts as a connection between the realms of the earth and the sky. It is believed that the ash tree will be the first tree to be hit by lightening. In folklore, ash was referred to as a home for fairies. A staff of ash is hung over door frames for protection as it will ward off evil influences. Ash leaves scattered in the four directions will protect the house against witches and psychic attacks. Despite its role in protecting against witches, the ash is also used by them. The ash is their favourite tree for making ritual dolls into which they stick pins.

The ash is an important woodland and hedgerow tree in Ireland. Ash and oak are one of the last trees to come into leaf and, according to folklore, the one that comes into leaf first, gives us an indication as to what the weather will be like for the summer: 'Ash before the oak, you can expect a soak, but oak before the ash, expect a little splash.'

It is part of the triad of fairy trees. In folklore it is believed that fairies could be seen by mortals wherever oak, ash and hawthorn trees grew together.

If you place ash berries in a cradle, it protects the baby from being taken by the fairies. Sailors believe that if they carve a piece of ash wood into the shape of a solar cross and carry it with them then they will be protected from drowning.

A few ash leaves in your pocket will act as health charms and it was even believed that they could gain you the love of the opposite sex. Another belief was that burning ash wood at Yule would bring you prosperity (the Yule log). However, given the duality in all things, not all the ash tree merits are good. The ash tree was believed to have a particular affinity with lightning. So, according to legend, standing under an ash tree during an electrical storm would be even more dangerous.

Numerous uses of the ash tree for medicinal purposes are known. The bark, being very astringent, can act as an anti-periodic. Ash is also a recognised remedy for flatulence. Ash treatment can help alleviate rheumatoid arthritis and it may help restore order to the liver and spleen. Ash leaves are acclaimed for their laxative property and are used in herbal medicine for dropsy and obesity. Ash is also considered to be able to cure jaundice and dissolve stones.

It is believed that the leaf of the ash can be used to remove skin disorders such as warts or boils. It was said that if you carried a needle for three days and then drove it into the bark of an ash tree, then the skin disorder (wart) would disappear from the person only to reappear as a knob or small growth (wart) on the tree, an example of transference.

The ash is often found growing near sacred wells and it has been suggested that there is a connection between the tree and the healing waters of the well (possibly iron contained in the roots leeching into the well). The tree itself can sometimes supply the water. One such tree in Sligo has a hollow in it like a bowl and the water that gathers in this is well known for its healing properties. This could be a good example of a *Bile* tree (a sacred tree).

Folk uses of the ash involve some clear examples of the transference of disease. One custom, made famous by Gilbert White in the eighteenth century, was to make a so-called shrew-ash, by imprisoning a live shrew in a hole bored in an ash tree. This tree then maintained its medicinal virtue for its lifetime. Such trees were used as 'cures' for a variety of ailments, including whooping cough and paralysis. A hernia in children was thought to be curable by splitting open a growing ash sapling and passing the child through the opening. The tree was then bound up, and as it healed, so would the child. Ash sap was used to treat earache and another use was as an aid to weight loss – for this purpose, the dried leaves were used as a tea.

As well as making hurleys and spears, ash had a wide variety of uses, including for building, making fences, furniture and boats. The bark of the ash could be used for tanning and the dried leaves were sometimes used as fodder for livestock.

THE ROWAN

(*Caorthann*)

THE ROWAN'S MYTHIC ROOTS go back to classical times. Greek mythology tells of how Hebe, the goddess of youth, dispensed rejuvenating ambrosia to the gods from her magical chalice. When, through carelessness, she lost this cup to demons, the gods sent an eagle to recover it. The feathers and drops of blood which the eagle shed in the ensuing fight with the demons fell to earth, where each of them turned into a rowan tree. Hence the rowan derived the shape of its leaves from the eagle's feathers and the appearance of its berries from the droplets of blood.

In Ireland the rowan has a long association in folklore as a tree that protects against witchcraft and enchantment. The physical characteristics of the tree may have contributed to its protective reputation; one notable feature is the tiny five-pointed star or pentagram on each berry opposite its stalk (the pentagram being an ancient protective symbol). The colour red was deemed to be the best protection against enchantment, and so the Rowan's vibrant display of berries in autumn may have further contributed to its protective abilities, as suggested in the old rhyme: 'Rowan tree and red thread / make the witches tine [meaning 'to lose'] their speed'. The rowan was also known as a tree of the goddess or a fairy tree by virtue (like the hawthorn and elder) of its white flowers. An alternative name, 'quicken', refers to its 'quickening' or life-giving powers, while the Irish name *Caorthann* derives from the word *Caor*, which means both a berry and a blazing flame.

There are several recurring themes of protection offered by the rowan. The tree itself was said to afford protection to the dwelling by which it grew, and pieces of rowan would be hung in the house to protect it from fire. It was also used to keep the dead from rising and tied to a hound's collar to increase its speed. Sprigs of rowan were used as a protection for the cattle and against the supernatural forces that may threaten the dairy products. It was kept in the byre to safeguard the animals and put in the pail and around the churn to ensure the 'profit' in the milk was not stolen. We also find records of instances as late as the latter half of the twentieth century of people being warned against removing or damaging a rowan in the garden of their newly purchased house. It was traditionally planted in churchyards since it was considered a protection against evil.

The rowan is particularly associated with the month of May. At Bealtaine livestock would be driven between twin fires to keep away evil influences. Homes, crops and cattle were believed to be at risk on May eve. The first smoke from a chimney on May morning should be from a fire of rowan twigs; this was done to thwart any mischief that the witches might be planning. A piece of rowan was put in the crops for protection and cattle going out in the morning were struck with a switch of wood. On May eve it was also the practice to put a loop of rowan on the tails of livestock, especially cows, to protect them from the fairies. Also, on May eve sprigs of rowan were placed on windowsills, doorsteps and even the roof for protection.

The rowan's wood is strong and resilient, making excellent walking sticks, and is suitable for carving. It was often used for tool handles, and spindles and spinning wheels were traditionally made of rowan wood. Druids used the bark and berries to dye the garments worn during lunar ceremonies black and the bark was also used in the tanning process. Rowan twigs were used for divining, particularly for metals.

The berries can be made into or added to a variety of alcoholic drinks and different Celtic peoples each seem to have had their favourites. As well as the popular wine still made in the Highlands, the Scots made a strong spirit from the berries, the Welsh brewed an ale, the Irish used them to flavour mead and even a cider can be made from them. Today rowanberry jelly is still made in Scotland and is traditionally eaten with game.

Rowans are a species that are at home in some of the more challenging parts of our ecosystem, such as barren mountainsides. They are also one of the species that bear their male and female flowers on separate trees so that it is necessary to have both genders present in a population in order to produce viable seed.

The fresh flowers and the dried fruits are both used medicinally. They have laxative and diuretic properties that can be valuable in the treatment of arthritis and rheumatism. They are also used to treat menstrual pain, constipation and inflammation of the kidneys, and are also used as a gargle for sore throats. The berries are high in fruit acids, vitamin C and fruit sugars. The bark is used as a strong astringent to treat diarrhoea internally and to treat leucorrhoea as a wash.

The leaves and berries of the rowan are sometimes added to incense to aid divination and to increase psychic powers. It's believed that the bark and berries carried on a person will also aid in recuperation and they are added to health and healing sachets, as well as power, luck and success charms. Rowan wood has traditionally been used for making Druids' staffs and its branches used for dowsing or divining. Some believe magic wands made from rowan are especially effective in ritual when psychic intuition is required.

THE HOLLY

(Cuileann)

IN CELTIC MYTHOLOGY THE Holly King would reign supreme over the land from the summer to the winter solstice, then his brother the Oak King reined from winter to the summer solstice. During the solstice rituals, it has been suggested that Druids wore sprigs of holly in their hair; however, I very much doubt the validity of this suggestion.

Holly was thought to protect you from lightning so it was considered to bring bad luck to whoever cut down a holly tree. However, you were allowed to take branches into your home to bring protection to the household. An old superstition held that if the holly leaves brought into the home were prickly then the man would rule the house for a year; if the leaves were smooth then the woman would rule.

If a holly bush was found growing in a hedge, then it would be left alone for it was believed that when witches ran along the top of hedges the holly would prevent them from following their chosen path.

The Druids considered holly to be a sacred plant and a symbol of fertility and eternal life. It was thought that the holly had magical powers as most plants die down in winter; however, the holly, with its dark glossy leaves and red berries, remained green and vibrant right through even the coldest weather. The holly was brought indoors as it was thought to encourage the coming of light in a time when the dark days of winter were upon the land.

It has been suggested by historians that the Romans associated holly with their god of agriculture and the harvest, Saturn. They would decorate their homes and buildings with sprigs of holly during the festival of Saturnalia, which was near the winter solstice (21 December). The Romans also decorated their statues and carried holly in their processions. It has been suggested that it was the Romans who first gave gifts of holly wreaths and that the festival of Saturnalia is the festival that the Christian Church modelled Christmas on. It should be remembered though that Saturnalia, was not really a solstice festival as it began on 17 December, it lasted for three days but was later extended into five days and ended on 23 December.

The Christians believed that the holly symbolised Christ's suffering upon the cross; the holly berries were said to represent the blood of Christ shed during his crucifixion. The legend states that the holly berries were originally white but were stained by the blood of Christ, which he shed for the sins of humans in order to win salvation for them. The Christians also believed that the green holly leaves with their prickly edges were a symbol representing the crown of thorns placed upon the head of Christ. Some Christians also believe that the cross used for the crucifixion was made from a holly tree and that holly would spring up from wherever the risen Christ walked. Although it became associated with Christmas, the Church was not always keen on the idea. In the sixth century, Bishop Martin of Braga tried to put a stop to the practice, but it seems he was fighting a losing battle and holly became a major feature of Christmas symbolism and decoration. In the fifteenth century, evergreens were used widely. In Stow's *Survey of London* it was recorded that 'every man's house, as also the parish churches are decked with holm [holly], and ivy'. Holly is often found paired with ivy for decorations. In fifteenth-century London, wreaths of the two plants were placed upon poles in the streets at Christmas. Again, this is perhaps due to the scarcity of greenery during the winter.

The myth of the Oak King and the Holly King is well known among modern pagans. The basis of the story is that these two great kings represent the polar forces of the year, and that they are in eternal combat, with the Holly King triumphant in winter and the Oak King in summer. It is interesting to note that within folklore holly is also strongly connected to ivy: holly is said to represent the king whilst ivy represents the queen. The most famous example is to be found in the old carol 'The Holly and the Ivy'.

It was widely believed that cutting down a holly tree would bring bad luck. However, holly was brought into the home to protect those within from malevolent fairies, or to allow those fairies present to remain in the home without causing problems for the occupants during the winter. In Ireland, the holly was called the 'gentle tree' and it was said to be one of the favourite trees of the fairies. Sometimes, the doorframe of a house would be made of holly for the same reason. Holly trees and hedges planted around a house were also grown for their protective properties.

A good crop of berries is a warning of a hard winter ahead. However, it is also a good sign that we have had a great summer. Holly berries are poisonous to humans but a good winter food source for birds and livestock. Some farmers even ground the leaves down to make them easier to consume.

The wood from the holly tree was thought to control horses so whips were made from coppiced holly.

The leaves of the holly tree were used to treat colds and fevers largely associated with the winter months and, as a flower remedy, holly is said to rid people of jealousy and hatred and open the heart to love.

9

THE HAZEL

(An Coll)

THE HAZEL TREE WAS held in great esteem by the ancient Irish as it was believed to have many magical, powerful and mysterious properties. These properties were known only to the wise and adept and would give those who knew of the powers of the hazel protection against evil spirits and the fairy folk. The Irish Celts believed that by eating hazelnuts you would gain wisdom and poetic inspiration. There are several variations on an ancient tale that nine hazel trees grew at the head of the great rivers of Ireland, dropping nuts into the water to be eaten by some salmon (a fish held sacred by Druids). By eating the hazelnuts the salmon absorbed their wisdom. The number of bright spots on the salmon was said to indicate how many nuts they had eaten.

In one variation of this legend, one salmon was the recipient of all these magical nuts. A Druid master, in his bid to become all-knowing, caught the salmon and instructed his pupil to cook the fish but not to eat any of it. However, in the process, hot juice from the cooking fish spattered onto the apprentice's thumb, which he instinctively thrust into his mouth to cool. This gave him the fish's wisdom. The young man was called Fionn Mac Cumhail and he went on to become one of the most heroic leaders in Irish mythology. It was said that he only had to suck his thumb and he would gain knowledge of future events.

Many early Irish tales describe poets and seers as 'gaining nuts of Wisdom', which is most likely a metaphor for such heightened states of consciousness. It has been suggested that this may have been the result of drinking a rather potent brew made from hazel that could affect a person's mental state (psychotropic). There are many references to drinking 'hazelmead' in early Irish literature and of Druids eating hazel nuts to gain prophetic powers.

Druidic wands were made from hazel wood and it has always been the preferred wood for water divining and dowsing. Some young lovers might still roast hazel nuts over the fire at *Samhain/* Halloween. The way they burnt foretold the course of their relationship in the coming year; would they stay together or fly apart? The connection between hazels and love is a very ancient belief. An old Fenian story tells how Maer, the wife of one Bersa of Berramain, fell in love with Fionn and tried to seduce him with hazel nuts from the Well of Segais bound with love charms. Fionn refused to eat them, pronounced them 'nuts of ignorance' rather than nuts of knowledge and buried them a foot deep in the earth.

There are many Irish superstitions surrounding the use of hazel. For centuries it was used for protection against evil. No harm could penetrate a hurdle fence of hazel around a house or a breast band of the wood on a horse. A shipmaster wearing a cap into which hazel had been woven was guaranteed to weather any storm, while a hazel nut in a pocket warded off rheumatism or lumbago, which was thought to be caused by 'elf shot', and a double-nut prevented toothache. Cattle driven through Bealtaine and summer solstice bonfires had their backs singed with hazel rods for protection against disease and the evil eye, and the scorched rods were used to drive them the rest of the year.

In the legend of the early Celtic St Melor, an abbot gathers hazelnuts and offers them to the saint. On receiving them, his artificial hand becomes flesh and blood.

Hazel trees frequently grow together in small groups and you can still see hazel woods as you travel around the Irish countryside. They thrive in hedgerows, woods and scrubland and respond well to coppicing, a practice that can actually extend, and even double, the lifespan of the tree. It may be one of the reasons why we have continued to put the young shoots or whips and the thin trunks to a variety of uses.

Hazel is a fabulous wood from which to make staffs and wands for ritual Druidic use; it has also been used to make staffs for self-defence, or to make shepherds crooks and everyday walking sticks. The wood readily splits lengthways and bends easily, making it ideal for weaving wattle hurdles for use as fencing or walls when daubed with mud and lime. Like willow, young coppiced hazel shoots were used to weave a variety of baskets and other containers. Hazel stakes bent into a U-shape were also used to hold down thatch on roofs and forked twigs of hazel were favoured by diviners searching for water.

Hazel leaves are usually the earliest native leaves to appear in spring and often the last to fall in autumn and they were fed to cattle as fodder. There was also a belief that they could increase a cow's milk yield.

Tara, the chief seat of the kingship in Ireland, was built near a hazel wood, and the great monastery of Clonard was established in what must once have been a sacred pagan place known as the Wood of the White Hazel: Ross-Finnchuill.

One of the earliest Irish records of the use of herbs was after the battle of Magh Tura, County Mayo, between the Firbolgs and invading Tuatha Dé Danann. Baths of herbs were prepared into which the wounded were plunged. The Dé Danann had a great physician named Dianacht, who recommended a porridge consisting of hazel buds, dandelion, chickweed and wood sorrel boiled together with meal. This was used for the relief of colds, sore throat and worms up until the last century.

In Christian teachings, there is an old tradition that tells us that when God banished Adam from the Garden of Eden to live upon the earth he gave him certain powers. One of these powers enabled Adam to produce animals that he needed to help him exist upon the earth by striking the sea with a hazel rod. It is said that Adam tried this and produced a sheep. Eve wished to copy him but upon striking the water she produced a wolf, which immediately attacked the sheep. Adam struck the water once again and produced a dog, which attacked the wolf and chased it away.

There is also a legend that states that after eating the forbidden fruit, Eve hid herself in the foliage of a hazel tree. The hazel tree also gave shelter to the Virgin Mary as she travelled to Egypt to visit Elizabeth. Surprised by a sudden storm, it is said she gained shelter under a hazel tree.

Hazel rods or staffs seem to have a strong connection with pilgrims as they were often left in churches or even kept as relics and were buried with their owners. Several hazel staffs were found in Hereford Cathedral in England. There is even a legend that St Joseph of Arimathea built the original abbey of Glastonbury from hurdles of hazel branches.

An Irish tradition tells us that the hazel frightens serpents as St Patrick held a rod of hazel in his hand as he stood upon Croagh Patrick in County Mayo. It is said that it was upon this mountain that St Patrick fought the demons of Ireland in the shape of serpents and banished them from the country.

THE IVY

(Eidhneán)

DRUIDS REVERE THIS PLANT and often used it in their rites. The Latin name for ivy, *hedera*, derives from the Celtic word for 'cord'. In Irish folk medicine, the main use of ivy has been in the treatment of corns. However, burns and scalds were also treated with an ointment made from the boiled leaves and fat and it was also used to stop bleeding and reduce inflammation.

Like many other evergreens, it symbolises the concept of eternity – a belief in everlasting life and resurrection after death. Because it is often found growing on dead and decayed trees, it came to represent the immortal soul – which lives on even after the body has returned to the earth. Yet at the same time, because it was often found in sites of death (including cemeteries and old tombstones), it was also viewed as an emblem of mortality. In some old beliefs, if ivy fails to grow on a grave, it symbolises a restless soul; ivy growing abundantly on a young woman's grave indicates death from a broken heart.

Like holly, ivy is one of the plants found in the Celtic Tree Calendar, where it is known as *gort*. Perhaps it was the Celts who influenced the Roman ivy 'party head wreaths' … for the Druids would wrap their heads with ivy to represent clarity of thought. In ancient Egypt the ivy was sacred to Osiris, and a safeguard against evil.

The botany of the ivy plant has clearly influenced its symbolism: amongst its various meanings, ivy represents connections and friendships, undoubtedly influenced by the plant's natural tendency to weave and intertwine during growth. Such connections often play an important role in our celebrations as we reach out to family and friends, to recall cherished memories and create new ones.

Ivy was used in love divination at Samhain, as recalled in an Irish rhyme:

> Nine Ivy leaves I place under my head
> To dream of the living and not of the dead
> To dream of the man I am going to wed
> To see him tonight at the foot of my bed.

Ivy was also used for death divination at Samhain. You nominate an unblemished leaf for each member of the family; each person puts their leaf in a glass of water to stand overnight. In the morning if the leaf was still unblemished then you were sure of life for the next year. However, if your leaf had spots on it then you would not see the next Samhain.

The following is an old Irish story about ground ivy.

The Fairy Dance

One evening late in November, which is the month when spirits have most power over all things, as the prettiest girl in all the island was going to the well for water, her foot slipped and she fell. It was an unlucky omen. When she got up and looked round it seemed to her that she was in a strange place and all around her was changed as if by enchantment. At some distance she saw a great crowd gathered round a blazing fire and she was drawn slowly on towards them, until at last she stood in the very midst of the people; but they kept silence, looking fixedly at her, and she was afraid. She tried to turn and leave them, but she could not. Then a beautiful youth, like a prince, with a red sash and a golden band on his long yellow hair, came up and asked her to dance.

'It is a foolish thing of you, sir, to ask me to dance,' she said, 'when there is no music.'

Then he lifted his hand and made a sign to the people and instantly the sweetest music sounded near her and around her. The young man took her hand, and they danced and danced till the moon and the stars went down, but she seemed like one floating on the air, and she forgot everything in the world except the dancing, and the sweet low music and her beautiful partner.

At last the dancing ceased and her partner thanked her, and invited her to supper with the company. Then she saw an opening in the ground and a flight of steps. The young man, who seemed to be the king amongst them all, led her down, followed by the whole company. At the end of the stairs they came upon a large hall, all bright and beautiful with gold and silver and lights. The table was covered with everything good to eat, and wine was poured out in golden cups for them to drink. When she sat down they all pressed her to eat the food and to drink the wine; and as she was weary after the dancing, she took the golden cup the prince handed to her, and raised it to her lips to drink. Just then, a man passed close to her, and whispered, 'Eat no food and drink no wine, or you will never reach your home again.'

So she laid down the cup and refused to drink. This angered them, and a great noise arose. A fierce, dark man stood up, and said, 'Whoever comes to us must drink with us.'

He seized her arm and held the wine to her lips, so that she almost died of fright. But at that moment a red-haired man came up and he took her by the hand and led her out.

'You are safe this time,' he said. 'Take this herb and hold it in your hand till you reach home and no one can harm you.' And he gave her a branch of a plant called the *Athair-Luss* (ground ivy). This she took and fled away along the sward in the dark night; but all the time she heard footsteps behind her in pursuit. At last she reached home and barred the door, and went to bed. But a great clamour arose outside and voices were heard crying to her, 'The power we had over you is gone through the magic of the herb; but wait – when you dance again to the music on the hill, you will stay with us for evermore and none shall hinder.'

However, she kept the magic branch safe and the fairies never troubled her more; but it was a long time before the sound of the fairy music that she had danced to that November night on the hillside with her fairy lover left her ears.

11

THE HONEYSUCKLE

(*Féithleann*)

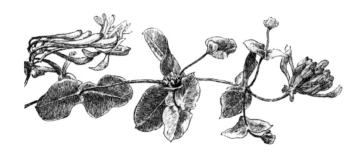

OTHER NAMES FOR HONEYSUCKLE include Irish vine, woodbine, fairy trumpets, honeybind, trumpet flowers, goat's leaf and sweet suckle. The old name, woodbine, describes the twisting, binding nature of the honeysuckle through the hedgerows. It was believed that if honeysuckle grew around the entrance to the home it prevented a witch from entering. In other places it's believed that grown around the doors it will bring good luck. If it grows well in your garden, then you will be protected from evil. In Ireland honeysuckle was believed to have a power against bad spirits, and it was used in a drink to cure the effects of the evil eye.

Bringing the flowers into the house will bring money with them.

Honeysuckle has long been a symbol of fidelity and affection. Those who wear honeysuckle flowers are said to be able to dream of their true love. In the language of flowers, its clinging nature symbolises, 'we are united in love', and emphasises the bond of devotion and affection between two people. It was also believed that if the blooms were brought into the house then a wedding would follow within a year.

In the Victorian era, there was a ban on young girls bringing honeysuckle into the home because the heady fragrance of the flowers was believed to cause dreams that were far too risqué for their sensibilities.

The wood has been incorporated into walking sticks because of its tendency to grow around and entwine saplings. The dried flowers are used for pot-pourri, herb pillows and floral waters. Also, scented cosmetics are made from the fresh flowers.

A lesser-known fact about the honeysuckle family is that *Lonicera tatarica Tatarian*, a leggy bush honeysuckle with sweet-scented pink flowers, is used as a substitute for catnip. The wood contains nepetalactone, which is the active ingredient found in catnip.

The leaves and flowers of the honeysuckle are rich in salicylic acid, so they may be used to relieve headaches, colds, flu, fever, aches, pains, arthritis and rheumatism. The leaves have anti-inflammatory properties and contain antibiotics active against staphylococci and coli bacilli. Honeysuckle flowers and flower buds are used in various infusions and tinctures to treat coughs, catarrh, asthma, headaches and food poisoning.

Pounding together two plants, woodbine and maiden-hare, then boiling them in new milk along with oatmeal will cure dysentery when ingested three times daily.

In the ancient laws of Ireland, which were called Brehon Law, trees and shrubs were protected because of their importance to the community. Penalties were imposed on anyone that damaged them unlawfully. There were four classes of tree/shrub; these were the nobles of the wood, the commoners of the wood, the lower divisions of the wood and the bushes of the wood. Their importance and placing within a group depended upon their worth within the community. This was related to their use, type of timber. Size or whether it bore fruit. Honeysuckle was placed in the group lower divisions of the wood. It was also linked by some medieval scholars with the ancient Irish Ogham alphabet.

Please note that honeysuckle berries are highly toxic and should NEVER be used on any count.

12

THE MEADOWSWEET

(Airgead Luachra)

A CREAMY, PERENNIAL OF damp waysides, meadows, marshes and woods, this tall, hairless plant flowers throughout Ireland from June to September. Its heavy fragrance is evocative of summer days in the countryside and legend says that meadowsweet was given its fragrance by the land goddess Aine. Bees frequently visit the flower heads. However, in spite of this fragrance, the flowers produce no nectar, but are heavy with pollen so the insects' visits serve to fertilise the plants. A peculiarity of this flower is that the scent of the leaves is quite different from that of the flowers, the leaves having a heavy almond-like aroma whereas the flowers have a strong sweet smell.

Meadowsweet's herbal uses had a base in scientific fact, in common with many other folk and herbal remedies. In the nineteenth century, chemists isolated salicylic acid from meadowsweet. The acid is a disinfectant so it not only made rooms smell better but also helped fight against bacteria. In Ireland it was used to scour milk vessels.

It is a painkiller and anti-inflammatory but hard on the stomach. Only after it was synthesised did it become an acceptable candidate for mass production and sold in tablet form as 'aspirin' –

'a' for acetyl and 'spirin' for spirea, the original botanical name for meadowsweet. It is one of the three herbs considered sacred by the Druids; the other two are vervain and water mint.

Meadowsweet comes from the Anglo-Saxon *'meodu-swete'*, meaning 'mead sweetener' and it was historically used to flavour mead (one of its other names, mead wort, also stems from this use). Cooks also used the herb to flavour beers and wines and added it to soups for an interesting almond flavour. The fresh leaves can be used to flavour sorbets and fruit salads. Infuse the flower to make a mild diuretic tea – but let it steep to bring out the salicylic acid before serving. As a cosmetic, it was soaked in rainwater and used as astringent and skin conditioner.

It was also known as Bridewort because it was strewn on the ground at handfastings for the bride to walk on (*'wort'* is an old word that means herb or root) and it was also used in wedding posies and bridal bouquets. This plant was given to Cúchulainn in liquid form and it was said to calm his fits of rage and outbreaks of fever and it may be for this reason that another name for meadowsweet in Ireland is Cúchulainn's Belt or *Crios Conchulainn*. It is also associated with death as the scent of its flowers was said to induce a sleep that was so deep it was fatal. However, in County Galway it was believed that if a person was wasting away because of fairy influence then putting some meadowsweet under the bed ensured that they would be cured by the morning.

In some places the flowers were dried and smoked in a pipe (probably less damaging than tobacco). Meadowsweet was also spread on the floor in medieval times to provide a nice smell and deter insects.

Its roots produce a black dye and its leaves a blue pigment and yellow is obtained from the top of the plant. All of these dyes were used by the Celts.

13

THE GORSE, FURZE, WHIN

(Aiteann)

THE THORNY NATURE OF the plant means that it is often viewed as having protective powers. The flowers are a deep yellow and have a pungent coconut scent. Although the main flowering period is from March to August, flowers can be found on bushes throughout the year. There are three species of furze, which all have slightly different flowering seasons, so that to the casual observer it would appear that the bush is almost always in bloom. This lengthy flowering led to the country saying: 'when the gorse is out of blossom, kissing is out of fashion.' The habit of adding a sprig of furze bloom to a bridal bouquet is thought to allude to this, the all-year-round blossom being a symbol of continuous fertility.

It was popular with bakers, to whom it was sold as fuel for their ovens. It has a high concentration of oil in its leaves and branches and so catches fire easily and burns well, giving off a heat almost equal to that of charcoal. Older plants can carry a lot of dead wood, so furze can be a hazard in hot, dry summers. The ashes have high alkali content and can be mixed with animal fat to produce soap, or clay, to form a soap substitute. They were also spread onto the fields to improve the soil.

Furze can also be used as fodder for animals. It was said that an acre of furze could provide enough winter feed for six horses. It has half the protein content of oats. Horses and goats can strip the leaves and eat them straight from the plant, but it was usual practice to run the branches through stone mills or hit them with wooden mallets. This crushed the thorns and reduced the wood to a moss-like consistency, which made it more palatable, especially to cows and sheep. The bushes were often deliberately burnt down in order to encourage new growth, the fresh sprouts of furze and grass providing easily accessible food for stock.

Get a few handfuls of the yellow blossoms of the gorse and boil them in water. Give a dose of the water to a horse and it will cure worms.

In Ireland the flowers were also used to flavour and add colour to whiskey and the Vikings were reputed to have used them to make beer. They can also be used to make wine and tea.

Studies in the nineteenth century confirmed that the high alkaline content of the plant had a purgative effect. An infusion of the blooms, as a drink, was given to children suffering from scarlet fever. It was also used to cleanse the home; when sprinkled onto dirt floors, the smell of the plant was believed to kill insects, particularly fleas.

In homeopathy gorse is used to help people who have given up hope, who have no faith in the future. It puts people in touch with their own inner resources and helps them move forward by releasing courage and determination.

As one of the sacred trees, furze was included in the Celtic Bealtaine bonfires. The stock would be herded between these for purification and protection before being released onto the summer grazing. When this tradition diminished, torches of furze were still carried around the herds and farm buildings in order to cleanse the air and protect the animals against sterility.

Gorse is closely associated with the sun god Lugh, the Celtic god of light and genius and with the spring equinox, at which time it's one of the only plants in full flower. However, folklore attaches it to festivals throughout the spring and summer months as a symbol of the power of the sun. In Brittany the Celtic festival of Lughnasdagh, on 1 August, is known as the Festival of Golden Gorse.

As an evergreen that flowers the whole year round, furze is seen to carry within it a spark of the sun's life-giving energy, a spark that can be seen even through the darker winter months. It is a symbol of encouragement and a promise of good things to come. Furze tells us to remain focused and optimistic, even in the darkest days, to keep hopeful and remain constant throughout the inevitable periods of difficulty we all experience.

As one of the first spring flowering plants, the furze provides a plentiful supply of pollen for bees when they first come out of hibernation. The product of the bees' labour, honey, is the Celtic symbol of wisdom, achieved through hard work and dedication. The furze tells us that if we apply ourselves and keep faith in the future, we will be rewarded. However bleak things may appear, there is always the possibility of periods of fertility, creativity and well-being. Its thorns remind us that it offers protection from unwanted ideas or influences.

In Ulster eggs were dyed yellow by boiling them in water with furze blossom. The eggs were then used in Easter games and then eaten. In other parts of the country, the blossom and bark was used to dye clothes yellow while the young shoots were used to make a green dye.

A sprig of furze was kept in the thatch, over the door or under the rafters, to bring luck into the home. In some places it was wrapped around the milk churn or butter at May time to protect it from the fairies. If you wear a piece of gorse/furze in your lapel, you will never stumble.

The presence of furze on waste ground raises its value and in Irish law furze was considered one of the *Losa fĕdo* or 'bushes of the wood'.

The Pot of Gold

Sean Kelly lived alone; he had no wife as no girl in her right mind would marry him because he was lazy, dirty-looking, and smelly. He was the sort of fellah that thought hard work was meant for everyone else but not for him. His neighbours kept their land neat, well tended and fenced but his fields were full of weeds, his gates were broken and his fences and hedges untended, allowing his cattle to roam the roads

Sean spent his time daydreaming. You see, he had great plans, believing that one day he would be rich and have everything he needed or wished for. Lady Luck was definitely going to smile on Sean Kelly, or so he believed.

One Sunday morning Sean got up early, which was unusual for him but as it was a feast day he had decided the night before that he would walk into the nearby town where there was going to be sports, dancing, and drinking. He put on his only suit, which was a bit smelly but he didn't notice as he stank anyway, then he put on his best silk tie, waved a comb at the bit of hair he had left and looked in the mirror.

'Oh, what a treat for the young ladies,' he said and he smiled, revealing that the few teeth that he had left were all yellow and broken. Sean opened his cottage door and set off on the long walk into town. He passed by his own fields and it didn't seem to bother him that they were very sorry-looking compared to his neighbours' fields, which were full of lush green grass and healthy-looking cattle. On the contrary, he felt sorry for his neighbours as they were always slaving away, even today when he was on his way to enjoy the day's festivities.

As Sean walked along the road, he noticed that one of his shoe-laces had become undone so he bent down to tie it. Suddenly he heard a noise, 'Tic tack tic tack'.

It seemed to be coming from behind the hedge that ran along the side of the field he was passing but what was it? He listened again and once again he heard it, 'Tic tack tic tack'.

Sean was very puzzled. What on earth was it? Maybe it was a grasshopper, but no, this sound was louder and sharper. Could it be a thrush smashing a snail's shell against a stone? No, he thought, this sounded very different. Sean stood up and looked through a small gap in the hedge. What he saw nearly caused him to fall into the ditch. There, in the middle of the field, sat the smallest man he had ever seen. He was wearing a red hat with a white feather in it, green trousers and a yellow jumper. He was also wearing a leather apron. Sean nearly swallowed his broken teeth in surprise for what he was looking at was a leprechaun.

Sean gave a big grin; here was the bit of luck he had been waiting for. Straightening his tie, he climbed through the hedge, ripping his smelly suit on the briars and gorse, but it didn't matter because he would soon have all the money he would ever need and he would be able to buy a hundred new suits if he wanted, or so he thought. The leprechaun looked up as Sean stepped into the field.

'Good morning to you Sean, are you headed into town for the festivities?' asked the little leprechaun.

'I was but then I heard you tapping away so I thought I'd just stop to say hello,' replied Sean.

'Well, you're very welcome,' said the leprechaun, for he was very polite. 'Why don't you sit down and have a rest? There's a lovely little rock there behind you.'

Sean was just about to turn to look for the rock when he remembered the old stories that said if you took your eyes off a leprechaun even for a second it would disappear never to be seen again.

'He's a crafty little fellah,' thought Sean. 'I'll have to be careful otherwise I'll lose everything.' So he stood where he was.

'That's a great little shoe you're making,' Sean said.

'It is indeed,' replied the leprechaun. 'There's going to be a great ball tonight and I'm making a pair of dancing shoes for the Queen of the Fairies.'

Sean had never seen anything so beautiful in his life.

'They're absolutely gorgeous,' he said, 'but it isn't a pair of dancing shoes I'm looking for, even a pair as lovely as those.'

'No, I didn't think it was,' sighed the leprechaun.

'No indeed,' said Sean. 'I'm after your pot of gold. Everyone knows that leprechauns have a huge pot of gold and I want it.'

'A pot of gold,' laughed the leprechaun. 'You're pulling me leg aren't you? Why do you think I'm sat here in the middle of a field making a pair of shoes while everyone else is enjoying the festivities?'

'Why you decided to work has nothing to do with me; I've never understood the need myself. But this is my field you're sitting in and I demand you hand over your gold immediately,' said Sean, a little annoyed.

'This is your field, is it? Well, you should be ashamed of yourself. Look at it. It is full of poisonous ragwort and all the seeds are blowing into your neighbours' fields. You must be bone idle,' said the leprechaun.

'How dare you!' roared Sean, who was now in a terrible temper. He had already heard complaints about the state of his fields from his neighbours and he didn't want to hear any from a little shoemaker.

'Now give me my pot of gold,' and he grabbed the little leprechaun in a vicious grip.

'Let me go,' squealed the leprechaun. 'You're hurting me. You're squeezing me that hard I'm meeting in the middle and I can't breathe.'

'I'll let you go when you show me where my pot of gold is,' roared Sean.

'All right, all right, keep your hair on, you haven't got much left anyway,' said the leprechaun. 'Just put me down and I'll show you.'

Sean threw him down onto the grass. The leprechaun's little red hat was squashed sideways and the feather was bent. The leprechaun scrambled across to a clump of ragwort.

'It's under here,' he said, in a sulk.

Sean looked at the ragwort and let out a groan. How was he going to dig that up out of the ground? The field was dotted with ragwort. If he left to get a spade the leprechaun would disappear and he'd never find the spot again.

Now, every time Sean started to think he began to sweat and this was one of those times. He reached down and began to loosen his tie when suddenly it gave him an idea. With a big grin he took off his tie and tied it around the ragwort.

'I'm going home to get a spade,' he said to the leprechaun. 'Will you give me your word of honour that you will not touch that tie?'

'I will and you need not worry. I promise you that I will not touch your tie,' said the leprechaun.

Sean may have been bone idle and lazy but he could move very quickly when he wanted to and he was back home in a few minutes, found his spade and was back at the field in a flash. However, when he reached the field he threw the spade to the ground. The leprechaun had gone and red ties waved cheerfully in the breeze from thousands of clumps of ragwort.

Sean didn't go to town that day; he spent it sewing the holes in his ripped old suit. Once or twice he thought he heard someone laughing but it may have been the wind coming down his chimney. He never bought himself a new suit, but he did have hundreds of new red ties to wear on his next visit to town.

14

THE BLUEBELL

(Coinnle Corra)

BELIEVED TO CALL THE fairies when rung, it was thought to be unlucky to walk through a mass of bluebells, because they were thought to be full of spells. It is also considered an unlucky flower to pick or bring into the house.

The Latin name for this flower is *Endymion*, who in mythology was the lover of the moon goddess Selene. The goddess put Endymion into an eternal sleep, so she alone could enjoy his beauty. Bluebells were said by herbalists to help prevent nightmares and were used as a remedy against leprosy, spider-bites and tuberculosis, but the bluebell is poisonous.

The gummy sap produced from its bulbs made it useful as a starch substitute. It was also used as glue for bookbinding (as it is so toxic it stops certain insects from attacking the binding) and setting the tail feathers on arrows.

The bulbs are extremely toxic and this toxicity may be the origin of the superstitious belief that anyone who wanders into a ring of bluebells will fall under fairy enchantment and die soon after. Other tales come from a time when forests where forbidding places. People believed that the bells rang out to summon fairies to their gatherings. Unfortunately any human who heard a bluebell ring would soon die.

However, not all the bluebell's folklore is quite so gloomy. Some believed that by wearing a wreath made of the flowers, the wearer would be compelled to speak only truth. Others believed that if you could turn one of the flowers inside out without tearing it, you would eventually win the one you love.

Bluebells found in hedgerows may indicate an ancient hedge as their presence is indicative of ancient woodland.

15

THE FOXGLOVE

(*Lus Mór*)

THE NAME DERIVES FROM the shape of the flowers, which resembles the fingers of a glove – 'folk's glove', meaning that they belong to the fairy folk. Folklore tells that bad fairies gave the flowers to the fox to put on his feet to soften his steps whilst hunting. The whole foxglove plant is extremely poisonous, but provides a source of digitalis used by doctors in heart medicine.

The foxglove was believed to keep evil at bay if grown in the garden, but it was considered unlucky to bring the blooms inside. The commonest colour for the foxglove is pink, but you often see white blooms in the hedgerows.

In Irish folklore it was said that if a child was wasting away then it was under the influence of the fairies (fairy stroke) and foxglove was given to counteract this (it was known to revive people). One such remedy was the juice of twelve leaves taken daily. It could also work for adults; such a person would be given a drink made from the leaves and if they were not too far gone they would drink it and get sick but then recover. However, if they were completely under the spell of the fairies, then they would refuse to drink.

An amulet of foxglove could cure the urge to keep travelling caused by stepping onto the fairy grass, the 'stray sod' or *fód seachrán*. In Ireland it is believed that the foxglove will nod its head if one of the 'gentry' (fairy folk) passes by.

16

THE BRAMBLE/ BLACKBERRY

(*Dris*)

AN ALTERNATIVE NAME FOR blackberries is *Sméara Dubha*. They should not to be eaten after Samhain because the Púca/pooka spits on them and they become inedible (in some parts of Ireland they believe that the Púca/pooka urinates on them).

An arch of bramble which had rooted at both ends was believed to have special powers and if you wished to invoke evil spirits you could do so by crawling through the arch at Samhain while making your wish. An arch of bramble could also be used to cure; for example, a child with whooping cough could be cured by passing it under the arch three times before breakfast for nine consecutive days while saying, 'in bramble, out cough, here I leave the whooping cough'.

If you found a piece of bramble attached to a cow's tail at Bealtaine it was considered suspicious as it meant someone was trying to put a spell on the milk.

The flower of the blackberry was a symbol of beauty to the Gaelic poets, and a well-known love ballad has the name '*Bláth na Sméar*', or 'Flower of the Blackberry'.

Bramble was classed as one of the bushes of the wood in the old Irish Brehon laws on trees and shrubs and you could be fined for cutting it.

Blackberries were traditionally eaten mashed up with oatmeal to make a tasty porridge. They were also used for making jam. The roots were used to make an orange dye. In Ireland the root of the bramble was used to make the core for hurling balls and for pipes and the long shoots were used for wickerwork and even for securing thatch.

Medical uses include using the leaves in a cure for diarrhoea in both cattle and people; it could cure dropsy and was considered to have fantastic curative powers for coughs and colds. It was also used for a variety of skin complaints such as scalds, burns, boils, shingles and spots.

The Pooka/**Púca**

Here in Ireland the pooka is believed to be an animal spirit and it has been suggested that the name originated from *poc*, which means 'he-goat' in Irish. Another suggestion is that the name may come from the Scandinavian *pook* or *puke*, meaning 'nature spirit'. Whatever its origin, there is no mistaking that the pooka is a changeling that can take many different forms, human or animal, horse, donkey, goat, dog, cat or bull. Sometimes it has been described as a handsome young man or a beautiful young woman. When in animal form the pooka is usually jet black with fiery red or yellow eyes.

The pooka is said to live in the hills and mountains and, depending on where you live, it can be helpful or menacing. It has been known to help farmers or cause havoc depending on its mood at the time. It is cunning and deceitful and because of this it has also been called the trickster. Because of its power to create or destroy it has also been looked upon as a fertility god and through its use of human speech a prophesier.

In Irish folklore it often appeared as a horse that galloped across the countryside at night, destroying hedges, knocking down fences and gates, trampling crops and scattering livestock. It was said that while in this form the pooka liked to take its rider, usually a drunk, on a wild ride all night then throw them to the ground in the early morning. This person, already heavily inebriated, would have been under the spell of the pooka and would have no recollection of what had happened. This often accounts for the reason some people who, having gotten very drunk, report that they have no idea what happened the previous night. If you believe that, then you'll believe anything.

The only one to ever ride a pooka successfully was Brian Boru, the High King of Ireland. He gained control over the creature through the use of magic. He used a special bridle that contained three hairs of the pooka's tail and together with his physical strength he was able to stay on its back until the exhausted pooka surrendered. The High King then forced it to agree to two promises: first, that it would no longer torment Christian people and destroy their property and second that it would never again attack an Irishman (or woman), except those that were drunk or had evil in their heart. The pooka agreed but very shortly afterwards reverted to its old ways. After all, the pooka's master was the Prince of Lies, commonly called the devil.

In County Down, the pooka assumes the shape of a small, deformed goblin who demands a share of the crop at the end of the harvest and some people in that area suggest that it is for this reason that they place a corn dolly in the field when the crop has been cut. This is known locally as the Pooka's Share. In County Laois it takes the shape of a huge hairy bogeyman who terrifies those abroad at night; in counties Waterford and Wexford, it is said to appear as an eagle with a gigantic wingspan and in County Roscommon it is a large black goat with curling horns. In County Mayo the sight of the pooka can stop hens laying or cows giving milk and of course it stops me picking blackberries.

17

THE WILD STRAWBERRY

(*Sútalín*)

AS YOU WALK ALONG a *boreen* (a narrow rural road in Ireland, just wide enough for one cow to pass along), you may see wild strawberry plants growing in the hedgerow. These plants have flowers with five petals that are borne on short, hairy stalks. The flowers bloom from April to July and precede tiny, sweet fruits. They are members of the *Rosaceae* family (Rose), which are known for their love-inducing qualities.

The folklore of the strawberry is connected with fertility and love and it is said that when shared with another it will ignite feelings of love. So be careful who you share a strawberry with, especially a double strawberry, for you may be destined to fall deeply in love with one another.

Henry VIII's second wife, Anne Boleyn, was accused of witchcraft because she had a strawberry-shaped birthmark on her neck.

The wild strawberry is used medicinally in the treatment of fever, rheumatism and gout. It has also been used as a tooth whitener and to soothe sunburn. It makes a delightful tea and is a very good source of vitamin C and can aid the digestive process.

It is said that strawberries symbolised righteousness and perfection. Because of this, medieval stonemasons often carved a strawberry onto church altars and other stonework in churches. One of the reasons the strawberry was considered to have a spiritual connection was due to the structure of the leaves; they are trifoliate and early Christians thought they represented the Holy Trinity. In Victorian times, the strawberry symbolised perfection and sweetness in life and character. It was also thought to represent modesty because the berries are often found hiding under the leaves.

However, in the twelfth century, an abbess named Hildegard of Bingen (later to become a saint) declared strawberries unfit for consumption because they grew along the ground where snakes and toads could crawl upon them. Her words had a huge effect on local political figures of the time so they too declared the strawberry unfit and discouraged the population from eating the berries. This belief held sway for a number of years; however, strawberries were served at important political and social events as it was once believed that they brought prosperity and peace.

Within the pagan tradition, the three leaves of the strawberry plant also represent the three-fold earth or mother goddess. In Norse mythology, the sacred fruit of Freya, a strong and passionate goddess who symbolises love, fertility, fruitfulness and war, is the strawberry. There is a legend that tells us that Freya gives strawberries to the spirits/souls of children when they die so they may enter the afterlife.

They are said to hide within the fruit and are transported to heaven by Frigg, wife of Odin. This story is echoed in the Native American tradition, where it is believed that the wild strawberry is a special gift of creation to both children and women.

The Strawberry in Winter

One story told concerning strawberries is very similar to the story of Cinderella and it is called 'Strawberries in Winter'. Once upon a time, long, long ago, there was a rich man who had a beautiful wife and daughter. However, his wife died in a fatal accident, leaving him to raise his daughter on his own.

Eventually, he met and married a woman whose husband had also died and she too had a daughter. At first all seemed to go well; on the surface everything appeared normal and happy but what the rich man and his daughter didn't realise was that the woman he had married was an evil, scheming witch and her daughter was just as bad. It wasn't long before the rich man became ill, an illness he did not recover from. He quickly passed away, leaving his daughter in the clutches of her evil step-mother. She was forced to do all the housework and dirty jobs while her step-sister lived the life of a lady, entertaining suitors and searching for a prospective husband. Unfortunately for the daughter, her beauty was soon appreciated by the visiting suitors and they became uninterested in the rather ugly step-sister. This did not go down well with either the step-mother or step-sister so they decided that the daughter had to be disposed of.

They hatched a plan that entailed sending the daughter on impossible missions such as gathering violets, apples and strawberries in the dead of winter. Their hope was that she would get lost in the forest and freeze to death. Every time she became lost and began to suffer from the freezing cold, she prayed to the four seasons for help. Each time she prayed, the four seasons would appear in human form, sitting around a fire. They would invite her to sit and warm herself by their fire and then they would help her gather whatever she had been sent out to get in order that she may return home.

The evil pair sent her out to get two apples and of course she eventually returned home with two apples. The step-mother and step-daughter ate the apples but could not understand how the daughter managed to complete each mission and return home safely. They decided to go out themselves and collect more juicy red apples. Eventually they came upon the four seasons sitting around their campfire; instead of asking for permission, the evil pair were extremely rude to them and sat down by the fire and began helping themselves to whatever they want.

The four seasons realised who this pair must be and called upon the storm, wind, ice and snow and the evil pair were never seen alive again. So this story tells us that it is better to be like the daughter and the wild strawberry: modest and sweet in both life and character.

18

THE COW PARSLEY

(*Peirsil Bhó*)

ALSO KNOWN AS DEVIL'S parsley, possibly because of its resemblance to the highly poisonous hemlock, this plant appears in accounts of witchcraft practices. It is a native plant belonging to the *Apiaceae* family. It also goes by the names wild chervil, hedge parsley, keck, wild beaked parsley, Queen Anne's lace and mothers-die).

The name Queen Anne's lace dates from a time when Queen Anne travelled the countryside in May, around Kensington in England, in the hope the fresh air would alleviate her asthma. The roadsides were said to have been decorated for her by this plant.

As she and the ladies-in-waiting walked, they carried lace pillows; the cow parsley resembled the lace.

The origin of the name mothers-die seems to be a folk tale that children were told, which held that if they picked cow parsley, their mother would die. This threat would deter children who couldn't tell the difference between cow parsley and hemlock, which is poisonous.

The Celts used to include cow parsley in their diet, according to archaeologists who analysed the stomach contents of a Celtic man discovered in a peat bog in Cheshire. They also found emmer and spelt wheat, barley, fat hen and dock.

While some claim that the root of the wild plant is also edible, it is not advisable to eat any part of this plant unless it has been expertly identified. There are several plants that look the same as cow parsley and are extremely poisonous and potentially fatal if ingested, so do not eat this plant.

Cow parsley is said to get rid of stones and gravel in the gall bladder and kidneys but very little research has been done on the common plant. It has been used by amateur dyers as a beautiful green dye; however, it is not permanent. The most common use for the stalks is as pea-shooters as the stems are hollow, so children love them. The foliage used to be sold by florists in Victorian times and used in flower arrangements.

Like sweet woodruff, cow parsley has the reputation of 'breaking your mother's heart'. This is said to have come about because the tiny white blossoms drop quickly. In the days before vacuum cleaners, the temptation for mothers to ban these work-generating posies from the house was understandable. This might explain the superstition which holds that cow parsley is 'unlucky indoors' and a 'harbinger of death'.

The cultivated relative of cow parsley, chervil, is a well-known herb, which when made into an infusion can be used in the treatment of water retention, stomach upsets and skin problems. It can be used to promote wound healing. Chervil water is used as a constituent of gripe water. Cow parsley may be used as a natural mosquito repellent when applied to the skin.

19

THE NETTLE

(*Neanntóg*)

IN IRISH FOLKLORE THERE are many uses for nettle. Three doses of nettles in the month of April was said to prevent any disease for the rest of the year. It was believed that if a person went to a graveyard, plucked a bunch of nettles that grew there and boiled them, then gave the water to a person suffering from dropsy, they would be cured. Fever could be dispelled by plucking a nettle up by its roots while reciting the names of the sick man and his family.

Nettles are recognised as a rich source of vitamin C and contain more iron than spinach. They make a very tasty soup but it is essential to pick them from a place where no chemicals or pollution could have affected them and to use only the upper leaves as the lower ones may contain irritants.

Nettles also contain anti-histamines, which are helpful to those with allergies, and serotonin, which is said to aid one's feeling of 'well-being'. If you suffer from intestinal worms then drink the water of boiled nettles and you will be cured. They can also lower blood pressure. A person suffering from rheumatism should lie upon a bed strewn with nettles and arthritic joints were sometimes treated by whipping the joint with a branch of stinging nettles. The theory was that it stimulated the adrenals and thus reduced swelling and pain in the joint. Recently it has been discovered that *lectin* found in nettles is useful in treating prostate enlargement and is widely prescribed for this in our times.

Nettles are reputed to enhance fertility in men. However, nettle can alter the menstrual cycle and may contribute to miscarriages so pregnant women should not use nettle. Stinging nettle may also affect the blood's ability to clot and could interfere with blood-thinning drugs. They can also act as a diuretic, so they can increase the effects of certain drugs, raising the risk of dehydration. Stinging nettle may also lower blood sugar, so it could make the effects of certain drugs stronger, raising the risk of hypoglycaemia (low blood sugar) – diabetics beware.

The nettle is significant among plants used as medicine by the Celts in that it was probably one of the most widely used due to its ability to prevent haemorrhaging and stop bleeding from wounds. They would have used it to treat the wounds their warriors received in battle.

Nettles have a place in ancient Celtic folklore. They were also known as 'devil's claw' and were believed to indicate the living place of fairies. Their stings were said to protect one from witch-craft or sorcery.

Turkey and other poultry (as well as cows and pigs) are said to thrive on nettles, and ground dried nettle in chicken feed will increase egg production.

Nettles left to rot down in water make a fantastic liquid fertiliser.

20

THE PRIMROSE

(Sabhaircín)

THE SYMBOL OF SAFETY and protection, in ancient times it was placed on the doorstep to encourage the fairy folk to bless the house and anyone living in it. A string of primroses on the first three days of May would guard the house as it was believed that neither fairies nor witches could pass over or under this string. It was also said that if you ate the blooms of the primrose you would see a fairy. A string of primroses would be placed on either the doorstep of the house or over the door. Placing over the door was usually done for the barn or outbuildings to protect the livestock from malignant forces. In modern Ireland the placing of primroses or flowers on the doorstep or window sills is now done to celebrate the Virgin Mary on May Day.

Both the cowslip and the primrose were thought to hold the keys to heaven and so were considered to be very sacred by the Celtic people. The primrose was the flower of love and the bringer of good luck, and was the symbol of the first day of spring and so was laid across thresholds to welcome May Day. It was also considered to be a bringer of great inspiration for poets, the flower of youth, birth, sweetness and tenderness.

Insects, in particular ants, play an important role in pollinating these flowers. The nectar is located at the bottom of the flower tube and the long thin body of the ant is perfectly designed to carry and deliver pollen from other primrose plants. The primrose family is also remarkable for the number of hybrids it produces.

The primrose has many medicinal uses and was important in the past as a remedy for muscular rheumatism, paralysis and gout and an infusion of the roots was used to cure headaches.

The leaves and flowers can be used either fresh or dried; the roots should be dried before use. Nicholas Culpepper (the seventeenth-century English botanist whose work on herbs is still recognized today) was aware of the healing properties of the primrose and said, 'Of the leaves of Primrose is made as fine a salve to heal wounds as any I know.'

The primrose was highly prized by the Celtic Druids and its abundance in woods, hedgerows and pastures made it an easily collectible plant. Primroses were often carried by the Druids during certain Celtic rituals as a protection against evil. The fragrant oil of the flower was also used by the Druids to anoint their bodies prior to specific rites in order that they might be cleansed and purified.

Primroses are loved by the fairies, so if you grow them don't let them die for if you do you will greatly offend the fairies and who knows what will happen. It was said that primroses bloomed in Tír na nÓg and that people returning from there always brought a bunch back with them as proof that they had been there.

Primroses were very important in rural areas, especially during the butter-making season that began in May. In order to encourage cows to produce a lot of milk, primroses were rubbed on their udders at Bealtaine. Primroses would also be scattered on the doorstep to protect the butter from the fairies. In Ireland on the eve of May Day (Bealtaine), Primrose balls were hung on cow's tails and bunches of primroses would be left in cowsheds to protect the cattle from witches.

Primroses were also associated with chickens and egg laying and it was considered unlucky to bring primroses indoors if the hens were hatching in the coop dresser within the house.

The flower was often used in medicine throughout the ages as it has similar properties to aspirin. It has always been known as a 'healing' plant, and because of this it was often used in foods. Even today it is known for its healing properties and is often drunk as a tea. In Irish folklore it was believed that rubbing a toothache with a primrose leaf for two minutes would relieve the pain. It was also used as a cure for jaundice (yellow fever) and an ointment would be made from certain herbs, including primrose and pig's lard, and this would be used on burns.

In the world of the flower essence, it is said to help heal those who have experienced the loss of a mother figure as a child. Victorians used to plant primroses on the graves of children.

21

THE DANDELION

(*Caisearbhan*)

THE DANDELION, WITH ITS white puffball head full of seeds, is known and loved by Irish children and is traditionally a symbol of hope, summer and childhood. However, dandelions are disliked by a number of gardeners who class them as weeds. There are many beliefs in Irish folklore involving the dandelion, some of which I've recorded here:

If you blow on the seed head of a dandelion whilst you make a wish then your wish will come true.

If an unmarried girl blows on a seed head and all the seeds blow off then her lover is true to only her. However, if a seed remains then he may not be as true as she thought.

If a married girl blows on a seed head then the number of seeds left upon it will indicate to her how many children she will have.

If you blow on a seed head and there are a number of seeds left it tells you how many years you have left.

If you blow on a seed head until all the seeds are gone, the number of puffs it took will tell you what time it is.

If you see seeds falling off the seed head and there is no wind then it means rain is on its way.

If you have a bad habit that you wish to rid yourself of, think about it as you blow on the seed head. As the seeds fly away they will take your bad habit with them.

If a child picks a dandelion flower off the plant then he will wet the bed.

The dandelion flower opens around 5 a.m. to greet the morning and closes in the evening around 8 p.m. to go to sleep

Dandelion is a rich source of vitamins A, B complex, C, and D, as well as minerals such as iron, potassium, and zinc. Dandelion leaves are used to add flavour to salads, sandwiches, wines and teas.

It was once believed that the leaves and root of the dandelion could be made into a tea that would aid the casting of spells or rituals concerning fortune telling, luck, calling spirits and making wishes, psychic powers, and wishes. If you put the flowers into a small red flannel bag and wear it around your neck, it will ensure all your wishes come true. Placing a couple of dandelion flowers into a wedding bouquet is believed to bring luck to a newly married couple.

It was said that it was good luck for a girl to wear a necklace of dandelions but only if it was she who made the necklace. It was bad luck if someone gave them to her.

It was unlucky to pick dandelions in a cemetery. It was even worse if you brought them home with you and a total disaster if you then gave them to someone else. However, it was OK if you picked them to lay them on a loved one's grave.

If dandelions appear in your dreams they represent a happy union.

The dandelion has long held a place in the medicine chest of the rural Irish. It was used in the treatment of indigestion, corns, scarlet fever, lip cancer and even heart trouble, as well as treating ailments including cuts, fractures, sore eyes, headaches, toothache, anaemia and diabetes. Pieces of the root, if worn as an amulet around the neck, were believed to cure cataracts.

The sap of the stem was used as a cure for warts while the leaves were dried and used to make a tea that aided digestion, while tea made from the root was used to treat insomnia, as a nerve tonic and as an aid to increasing a person's virility. A tincture brewed from the yellow flowers was believed to help with complaints related to the liver.

It is a natural diuretic and some people consider the roots the best laxative you could possibly use, while eating the dandelion was believed to improve the appetite of people who were suffering from tuberculosis and it was said that the leaves could even cure ulcers.

Some people would rub a dandelion flower between their hands and then rub the yellow on any area that ached. Many also used the leaf of the dandelion in much the same way as you would use a dock leaf to relieve the effects of a sting.

It isn't just humans who have relied upon the dandelion. Many wild birds eat the seeds as part of their staple diet. Bees used the plant as a source of nectar and many beekeepers will tell you that dandelion nectar produces some of the world's best honey. Pigs love the plant; however, horses won't touch it.

22

THE HEDGEHOG

(An Gráinneog)

THE HEDGEHOG GOT ITS name because of its peculiar foraging habits. As it moves through the hedges, it emits pig-like grunts, hence its name hedgehog. The hedgehog is called the *Gráinneog* in Irish, meaning 'little ugly thing'. However, it is not a native Irish mammal; many historians believe that it was introduced into Ireland around the thirteenth century by the Anglo-Normans, possibly as a food source. It is also thought that they used its spiny coat for carding/combing wool, a use shared by the ancient Romans.

There are many stories concerning the hedgehog. In the first century, Pliny the Elder, in his *Historia Naturalis*, told a story about how the hedgehog would climb apple trees, knock the fruit off, and then roll on the apples, impaling them on its spikes, and carrying them down to their burrows. Now not only do hedgehogs not climb trees but they don't store food in their burrows either. Although that didn't stop some people trying to prove he was right (they never succeeded).

In ancient Rome, the hedgehog was used to forecast the weather and the onset of spring. If during hibernation it looked out of its burrow around the start of February and saw its shadow then it meant there was a clear moon and this was believed to herald six more weeks of winter, so it would return to its sleep. German settlers in Pennsylvania brought folklore that associated the shadows of animals, including the hibernating hedgehog, with an extended winter. Hedgehogs aren't native to North America, but groundhogs are. They first emerge from their burrows in early February, just the same as hedgehogs. The settlers put two and two together and instead of a hedgehog they used the groundhog and a new strand of folklore was born.

In medieval Britain, farmers believed that hedgehogs stole milk from cows by sucking on them at night; they were even said to be witches in disguise. In 1566, the Elizabethan parliament put a three-pence bounty on the head of every hedgehog that was caught and killed. Even the Church got involved by offering bounties for each hedgehog killed. Hedgehogs certainly enjoy milk and some vets have reported damage to cows' udders, which may have been caused by hedgehogs, which have distinctive teeth marks, so it would appear that the odd hedgehog has had a nibble. Thousands were slaughtered as a result.

The poor hedgehog was then accused of being an egg thief. Now while it's true that they will eat the odd egg, most of these have already been cracked or damaged. It has been suggested that hedgehogs would actually find it difficult to break open an egg as they don't have the physical capability. However, thousands more were hunted down and killed as a result of this, a practice which is still carried out today, particularly on off-shore islands where the hedgehog feeds on the eggs of seabirds as this is really the only readily available food source.

The hedgehog has even been considered a food by some people. The common method of cooking them is to roll them in clay (spines and all); you then bake it in a fire. Once cooked, remove the hardened clay, taking the spines with it. At one time it was believed that eating hedgehogs would cure the sick of a variety of ailments, including leprosy, boils and even poor vision. It has been suggested that certain gypsies will still eat hedgehogs as a cure for poisoning and removing evil spells but I cannot swear to this.

The hedgehog was also worshipped by some cultures; some thought that a figure representing Mother Earth would take the form of a hedgehog. In particular, they were associated with the Babylonian goddess Ishtar (also known by her Greek name Asorte) who was the goddess of love and war. To the ancient Egyptians, the hedgehog symbolised reincarnation because they were said to have interpreted the hedgehog's hibernation cycle as death in autumn and rebirth in the spring.

Everyone knows what a hedgehog looks like – it's difficult to mistake it for anything else and its one of our cutest hedgerow mammals. It's about 10 inches long and has over 5,000 hard spines on its back. Muscles along the animal's back can raise and lower these spines to respond to threatening situations. When threat-ened, it will roll itself into a ball and these spines will protect it from most predators, except a determined badger or a hungry fox. Hedgehogs also have quite long legs and can run quickly when they have to – up to 6 feet per second. They have short tails, a good sense of smell and hearing but very poor eyesight.

They normally come out at night and eat slugs, worms and any little things they may find crawling around. In winter these food sources become scarce so the hedgehog has a clever way of surviving: it goes to sleep. This is called hibernation; their body temperature drops to match the surrounding temperature and their heart rate slows down from roughly 150 beats per minute to around 20 beats per minute. In November the hedgehog will find a sheltered spot and build a nest out of leaves and grass and there it will sleep until April – although they may wake up once or twice to go to the toilet.

Hedgehogs breed between May and October and the babies are born in summer. The female will be pregnant for about five weeks and she will give birth to between three and five babies in her nest in June or July. The babies are very vulnerable when born; their spines are soft, so they don't hurt the mother, and their eyes stay closed at birth so they are blind. However, after a couple of weeks their spines harden and their eyes open and when they are about six weeks old they are able to look after themselves.

It's very important not to disturb any animal that is hibernating unless they are in danger. Never go near a hedgehog nest, especially if there are babies in there as the mother hedgehog may decide to abandon the nest. If you would like to put a little food out for a hedgehog that may visit your garden, leave out some pet food as it is closer to their natural diet and much better than bread and milk.

They are famous for their fleas as their spines can hide large numbers of them. However, don't be worried: their fleas are only interested in hedgehogs and are harmless to humans and other animals.

Hedgehogs can swim but one of the common causes of hedgehog deaths is drowning; they fall into a pond or other source of deep water and cannot get out again because the sides are steep or slippery. (You can help the hedgehog and other wildlife by putting rocks or wire netting at the side of garden ponds.)

Hedgehogs can live up to six years but many are killed by cars or the effects of eating slugs killed by slug pellets. Others die from falling into cattle grids and, not being able to climb out again, starving to death and more than half of all hedgehogs die during hibernation due to cold, fire, flood, or someone wrecking their nest.

The Hedgehog and the Plum

Once upon a time, hundreds of years ago, Ireland was covered in trees and had many animals living wild that we just don't see roaming the countryside today: animals such as the bear, the wolf and the wild boar. It has been suggested that the hedgehog was brought to our shores by the Anglo-Normans as a food source and some of them may have escaped into the wild.

One day, a wolf, a fox and a hedgehog were passing the time of day talking to each other when they spotted a large group of humans coming their way, so they did what any right-minded animals would do and hid behind some trees. As the humans passed close by, a plum fell from a sack that one of the humans carried. The animals had heard about plums but had never seen one, let alone tasted one. They began to discuss which of them should have the privilege of eating this lovely juicy-looking fruit. However, there was only enough plum for one of them to eat.

After a long debate, the friends finally agreed to a contest. It was the wolf who had the idea: 'I know!' he cried. 'I think the one who gets drunk on poteen the quickest should have the pleasure of eating this plum!'

Thinking, of course, that he would win, the wolf continued: 'As for me, I get drunk after just one sip of poteen!'

The fox was next to speak and, knowing that he was much smarter than the wolf, he said, 'That's nothing! I get drunk just by smelling poteen!'

The last to speak was the hedgehog, whom the others looked down upon because he was so small. He told his friends: 'Well, its very sad for me, for I get drunk just by hearing about poteen!'

And with that, the hedgehog swayed as if he were drunk.

The other animals had to admit that this clearly made the hedgehog the winner. But before the hedgehog could open his mouth to eat his prize, the envious fox shouted, 'Wait! I have another idea. We need a second contest. I think that the one of us who runs the fastest should get to eat the plum!'

They all agreed to this second match and prepared themselves for the race. The hedgehog, who knew he stood no chance of winning because of his short legs, had already thought of a trick.

As the wolf and the fox took off in a cloud of dust, the hedgehog caught hold of the fluffy tail of the fox and held on tight.

Just before the speedy fox crossed the finish line, he stopped and looked back to check where the others were. At that moment, the little hedgehog dropped off his tail, scurried under his belly and, from the winning side of the finish line, called out, 'Well, hello there, Mr Fox! Hello Mr Wolf! I see you've finally arrived! What took you so long?'

And that is how the hedgehog won the contest.

As the wolf and the fox looked on, the clever little hedgehog gobbled up the plum. And you know what? A plum never tasted better.

The Hedgehog and the Hare

Once upon a time, on a beautiful summer's morning, the fields were full of flowers and the sun was shining down from a clear blue sky. There was a soft breeze blowing. The sounds of birdsong and the gentle humming of bees were in the air. All the creatures were happy, especially the hedgehog.

He was standing at the door of his little burrow with his arms crossed, singing a little song to himself, when it suddenly occurred to him: his wife was washing the children; the breakfast wasn't quite ready yet, so why not go for a little walk and check on his turnips? You see, the local farmer had planted the turnips close to his burrow and the hedgehog and his family were accustomed to eating them, so he considered them his own.

The hedgehog closed the door to his burrow and started down the path towards the turnip field. He hadn't gone far when who should he meet but the hare, who had decided that he would go for a walk and check his cabbage patch. When the hedgehog saw the hare, he wished him good morning but the hare was a bit of an arrogant sort and considered himself to be of a higher class than the hedgehog so he didn't return the greeting. Instead he said to the hedgehog in a very haughty and sarcastic voice, 'What are you doing running around so early in the morning?'

'I'm just out for a walk,' said the hedgehog.

'Out for a walk?' laughed the hare. 'I'd have thought you had better use for your little legs than that.'

Well, this made the hedgehog very angry, for he could stand anything except remarks about his legs – as everyone knows, the hedgehogs legs are very small and crooked.

'I suppose you have better use for your legs,' said the hedgehog.

'I should think I have,' said the hare.

'You think you're so clever,' said the hedgehog. 'But I bet if we were to run a race, I'd beat you.'

'That is a laugh! You, with your crooked little legs!' said the hare. 'But seeing how you're so eager, what would you bet?'

'My turnip field against your cabbage patch,' said the hedgehog.

'Accepted,' said the hare. 'Shake hands and we can start the race right away.'

'No, not yet. I've not had me breakfast,' said the hedgehog. 'I'm very hungry. First I want to go home and get something to eat. I'll be back here in about half an hour.'

The hare agreed and the hedgehog left.

On his way home the hedgehog thought to himself, 'The hare is relying on his long legs, but I'll still beat him. He may think he's a distinguished gentleman, but he's still a fool, and he'll be the one to lose.'

Arriving home, he said to his wife, 'Wife, get dressed quickly. You've got to go out to the field with me.'

'What's the matter?' said his wife.

'I bet our turnip field with the hare that I could beat him in a race and you should be there too.'

'My god, man,' the hedgehog's wife began to cry, 'are you mad? Have you entirely lost your mind? How can you agree to run a race with the hare?'

'Now, don't you be worrying,' said the hedgehog. 'Have I ever let you down before? Hurry up now, get dressed, and come with me.'

What was the hedgehog's wife to do? She had to go with him, whether she wanted to or not.

As they walked toward the field together, the hedgehog said to his wife, 'Now, here's the plan: we're going to run the race down the long field, the hare will run in one furrow and I'll run in the one next to it. We're going to start the race at the top end of the field. I want you to stand in at the bottom end of the field and when the hare approaches just shout out "I'm already here".'

When they arrived at the field, the hedgehog showed his wife where to hide, and then he went to the top of the field. When he arrived the hare was already there.

'Can we start?' said the hare.

'Yes, of course,' said the hedgehog. 'On your marks!'

Each one took his place in his furrow.

The hare counted, 'One, two, three', and he tore down the field like a rocket. But the hedgehog ran only about three steps and then ducked down in the furrow and remained sitting there quietly.

When the hare, arrived at the bottom of the field, the hedgehog's wife called out to him, 'I'm already here!'

The hare, startled and bewildered, thought it was the hedgehog himself, for, as everyone knows, a hedgehog's wife looks just like her husband.

The hare thought, 'Something's not right here.' He called out, 'Let's run back again!' And he took off again like a rocket, with his ears flying from his head. But the hedgehog's wife remained quietly in place.

When the hare arrived at the top of the field, the hedgehog called out to him, 'I'm already here!'

The hare, just couldn't understand it. He shouted, 'Let's run back again!'

'Fine by me,' answered the hedgehog. 'For all I care, we can do this all day if you want.'

So the hare ran seventy-three more times, and the hedgehog always kept up with him. Each time the hare arrived at the top or the bottom of the field, the hedgehog or his wife said, 'I am already here!'

But the hare did not complete the seventy-fourth time. In the middle of the field, he fell to the ground and surrendered.

The hedgehog took ownership of the cabbage patch he had won. When the hare had recovered and left the field in disgust, the hedgehog called his wife from her furrow and happily they went back home.

And ever since that time no hare has agreed to enter a race with a hedgehog.

The moral of this story is that no one, however distinguished they think they are, should make fun of others.

23

THE BADGER

(*Broc*)

SOME PEOPLE THOUGHT THAT badgers could bring bad luck. This rhyme dates from about 200 years ago:

> Should one hear a badger call,
> And then an ullot [owl] cry,
> Make thy peace with God, good soul,
> for thou shall shortly die.

Some people used to say that badgers had legs that were shorter on one side than the other. This was supposed to be because badgers often walked on sloping ground on the sides of hills. However, what would happen if the badger turned to face the opposite direction is not recorded.

Another 200-year-old story says that badgers – like black cats – can bring bad luck or good luck. If the badger walks across the path that you have just walked on, you are in for very good luck. However, if the badger walks across the path in front of you, and if it happens to scrape up a bit of earth as it goes, then it is time for you to choose your coffin! The old rhyme goes like this:

> Should a badger cross the path
> which thou hast taken, then
> Good luck is thine, so it is said
> beyond the luck of men.
> But if it crosses in front of thee,
> beyond where thou shalt tread,
> and if by chance doth turn the mould,
> Thou art numbered with the dead.

The badger was an animal that was always favoured by the gambling fraternity. Some gamblers were said to carry badgers' claws, teeth or hair to bring them good luck. If you wear a badger's tooth around your neck you will be lucky in whatever you place wagers on, especially cards.

Highlanders in Scotland, on the other hand, had rather more regard for the badger, admiring its strength and tough hide. This animal has a reputation for being unyielding in the face of danger and is noted for its tenacity and courage. Badger faces were, therefore, used to cover sporrans, badgers' teeth employed as buttons and badgers' penises were even given as fertility charms to bridegrooms from brides' fathers.

Badger fat was used for cooking and also rubbing on the chest as a cure for rheumatism. It was also used in the fifteenth century by witches who were said to have smeared it on their broomsticks in order to increase their speed and manoeuvrability.

Badger skin was made into bridles for horses in order to give the rider magical powers over the horse.

Henry Smith, author of *The Master Book of Poultry and Game*, which was published shortly after the end of the Second World War, declares 'the flesh can be treated as young pig in every respect, it being just as rich and having the flavour of a young pig'.

In the middle of the twentieth century, they were thought to be the carrier of tuberculosis, which was subsequently transmitted to cattle. Their persecution was relentless and their numbers in Ireland dipped as a result. Protection was afforded to badgers in the 1970s and since then their numbers have started to recover.

Their home, referred to as a 'set', is a complicated tunnel construction where the female or 'sow' raises up to three cubs each year during February or March. A badger set can be as much as 20 metres long and several metres below ground.

The badger is linked to perseverance, along with the patience and persistence this requires. He is considered self-reliant, determined, assertive and willing to work, with an earthy wisdom. *Brocan* was a name for Pictish wise men.

That said, the badger was not always treated with respect – the game 'Badger in the Bag' started, according to legend, with the Celtic hero Pwyll tricking a rival into a bag and each of his men having a turn at kicking the supposed 'badger' he had trapped. Bagging badgers before dealing with them (or indeed baiting them) also has to do with their aggression and fighting skills.

24

THE FOX

(*Sionnach*)

A POPULAR BELIEF CONCERNING the origin of the fox was that they were the dogs of the Norsemen who were supposed to have brought them to Ireland.

Foxes are very good at concealing themselves. Their ability to hide and move swiftly through the hedgerow corridors is legendary. It is this ability, together with their skill and cunning when it comes to taking poultry and small animals, that has resulted in the reputation they have today.

The Celtic Druids admired the fox for this skill and cunning. In 1984 the 2,000-year-old body of a man who had been garrotted was found in a bog near Manchester, England (Lindow man). He was wearing a fox-fur amulet and had traces of mistletoe pollen in his gut. His death, by three causes, led Dr Anne Ross to suggest that he may have been a Druid prince slaughtered in a ritual.

In common with the otter, the fox is said to carry a magical pearl, which brings good luck to whoever finds it.

The fox is associated with adaptability and was thought to be a shape-shifter. In folklore all over the world it's described as 'sly', 'clever', and 'cunning' – and not always to its credit. However, it should be remembered that 'cunning' comes from 'kenning', meaning 'to know', without necessarily denoting slyness. The fox is clever – it is clever at adapting so that it assimilates into its environment, even when this environment is changing rapidly.

That cunning includes leaving false trails in order to deceive its hunters – and foxes were hunted regularly for their pelts, perhaps in a ritual manner. Like the deer, the fox was often part of burial rituals, found now in excavations.

The fox was said to be able to foresee events, including the weather, and its barking was said to be a sure sign of rain.

It is thought to be unlucky to meet a woman with red hair or a fox when setting out in the morning, especially if you were a fisherman.

One cure for infertility was for a woman to sprinkle sugar on the testicles of a fox and roast them in an oven. She should then eat them before her main meal for three days in succession.

An Irish cure for gallstones and kidney stones was to rub the affected area with fox's blood. It was also believed to be a cure for gout and rheumatism.

The tongue of a fox was also thought to be able to remove a stubborn thorn from the foot, when all else had failed, and was also laid across the eyes to cure cataracts. A cooked fox tongue can be eaten to give person courage.

The dried and sweetened liver and lungs of a fox, if eaten, will cure a cough and if you finish a bowl of milk that has been licked by a fox it will cure whooping cough. The fat of a fox rubbed into your scalp will cure baldness while drinking fox droppings mixed with vinegar cures leprosy.

It was once believed that a fox troubled by fleas would swim into a river with a ball of wool or grass in its teeth. As the water rose, the fleas would climb along the body onto the head and finally onto the ball of wool or grass. The fox would then open its mouth and allow the ball to float away, taking the fleas with it.

Some farmers would nail a fox head to the door of their barn to scare away witches. This may be related to the idea that witches were able to turn themselves into foxes.

A fox seen near a house was said to be a symbol of impending disaster and if you were bitten by a fox, it was thought that you would die within seven years.

If it rains while the sun is shining, it means that a fox's wedding is taking place.

Brigid and the Fox

Brigid had a wonderful way with animals. One day a friend of the monastery workmen came to her with a sad tale that the friend had accidentally killed the king of Leinster's pet fox, thinking that it was a wild animal. The man was arrested. His wife and children had begged the king to spare his life, but to no avail, so the workman asked if Brigid would intercede for him.

Although Brigid loved animals, she thought it was wrong that a man's life should be demanded in return for the fox's, so she ordered her horse and cart to be made ready and she set out for the court. The way lay through a wood, where the road was a mere track and the horse had to walk. Brigid prayed for the right words to speak to the angry king to save the life of the woodsman.

Suddenly she saw a little fox peeping shyly at her around a tree and she had an idea. She told her driver to stop and called the animal to her. Immediately it sprang into the cart beside her and nestled happily in the folds of her cloak. Brigid stroked its head and spoke to it gently. The little fox licked her hand and looked at her with its big brown eyes.

When she reached the king's castle, the fox trotted after her. She found the king still in a mighty rage. 'Nothing,' he told her angrily, 'nothing in the world could make up or the loss of my beloved pet. Death is too good for that idiot who killed him. He must die as a warning to others. Let him die.'

The king stormed on, 'It is no use asking for mercy. That little fox was my companion and my friend. That idiot brutally killed him for no reason. What harm did I do to that man? Do you have any idea how much I loved that little fox? I cared for him from the first day he was born.'

The king's furious eyes met Brigid's loving ones. Yes, indeed, she could well understand it. She was truly sorry for his loss for she loved all animals and especially tame little foxes. Look here … She beckoned forward her new pet from the woods, which had been crouching behind her.

The king forgot his anger. He and his household looked on delightedly while Brigid proceeded to make the fox do all kinds of clever tricks. It obeyed her voice and tried so hard to please her that the onlookers were delighted. Soon she was surrounded by laughing faces.

The king told her what his own little fox could do. 'See, it used to jump through this hoop, even at this height.' Well, so could Brigid's. When the king's fox wanted a titbit, it used to stand on its hind legs with its forepaws joined as though it were praying. Brigid's could do the same thing. Could anything be more amusing?

When his mood had completely changed, Brigid offered her fox to the king in exchange for the prisoner's life. Now the king agreed and he even promised Brigid that he would not inflict any kind of punishment on that idiot workman, whose misdeed he would soon forget.

Brigid was very happy when the prisoner was restored to his wife and children and she went back home to the monastery. However, the little fox missed her and became restless and unhappy. It didn't care when Brigid led him into the castle, but without her the castle was a prison. After a while the king left on business and no one else bothered much about the new pet. The fox waited for its chance and when it found an open door, it made good its escape back to the woods.

Presently the king returned and there was commotion when the pet was missed. The whole household was sent flying out to search for it. When they failed to find the fox, the king's hounds were sent to help in the search, their keen noses snuffing over the ground for the fox's scent. Then the king summoned out his whole army, both horsemen and footmen, to follow the hounds in every direction. It was all no use. When night fell, they all returned wearily to their king with news of failure. Brigid's little pet fox was never found again.

So if you are walking through the woods one day and see a little fox with big brown eyes say 'hello'. You never know, it might be related to Brigid's fox.

25

THE RABBIT

(Coinín)

AND THE IRISH HARE

(Giorria Éireannach)

THE RABBIT AND THE hare are interchangeable in Irish folk-lore and are strongly linked to Ireland. The hare was immortalised as the animal gracing the Irish pre-decimal three-pence piece.

Hare mythology exists in almost every ancient culture and when the first settlers colonised Ireland, the Irish hare was already an iconic figure. There are many examples in Celtic mythology, and storytellers still relate tales of women who can shape-change into hares. Uses for the hare and rabbit were also abundant.

Placing a rabbit skin under your bed will bring fertility and abundance to your sexual activities. (If you're opposed to the use of real fur, use some other symbol of the rabbit that you're more comfortable with.)

The obvious one – a rabbit's foot is said to bring good luck to those who carry it, although one might argue that it's not so lucky for the rabbit.

To bring yourself boundless energy, carry a talisman engraved or painted with a rabbit's image.

If you have wild rabbits or hares that live in your yard, leave them an offering of lettuce, shredded carrots, cabbage or other fresh greens, as the wild rabbit is associated with the deities of spring.

Add a few rabbit hairs to a witch bottle for protection magic.

In some legends, rabbits and hares are the messengers of the underworld – after all, they come and go out of the earth as they please. It was believed that rabbits burrowed underground in order to better commune with the spirit world, and that they could carry messages from the living to the dead and from humankind to the fairies. If you're doing a meditation that involves an underworld journey, call upon the rabbit to be your guide.

Eostre, the Celtic version of Ostara, was a goddess associated with the moon and with mythic stories of death, redemption, and resurrection during the turning of winter to spring. Eostre was also a shape-shifter, taking the shape of a hare at each full moon; all hares were sacred to her and acted as her messengers.

Cesaer recorded that rabbits and hares were taboo foods to the Celtic tribes. In Ireland, it was said that eating a hare was like eating one's own grandmother – the 1893 edition of *Folklore* recorded that, 'Country people in Kerry don't eat hares; the souls of their grandmothers are supposed to have entered into them.' Perhaps this was due to the sacred connection between hares and various goddesses, warrior queens and female fairies, or else due to the belief that old 'wise women' could shape-shift into hares by moonlight.

The Celts used rabbits and hares for divination and other shamanic practices by studying the patterns of their tracks, the rituals of their mating dances, and mystic signs within their entrails.

As Christianity took hold in Western Europe, hares and rabbits, so firmly associated with the goddess, came to be seen in a less favourable light — viewed suspiciously as the familiars of witches, or as witches themselves in animal form and portents of disaster. A hare was a dreaded animal to see on a May morn. Hares were strongly associated with witches. The hare is quiet and goes about its business in secret. They are usually solitary, but occasionally they gather in large groups and act very strangely, much like a group of people having a conference. A hare can stand on its hind legs like a person; in distress, it utters a strange, almost human cry, which is very disconcerting to the listener. Watching such behaviour, people claimed that hares were actually witches who had changed their form. In this shape she stole milk or food, or destroyed crops. Others insisted that hares were only witches' familiars. Numerous folk tales tell of men led astray by hares who are really witches in disguise, or of old women revealed as witches when they are wounded in their animal shape.

An old Irish legend tells of a hare being spotted sucking milk from a cow on May Day morning. The hare was chased by hounds and received a bad wound and it made its way into an old house to hide. When the house was searched all that was found was an old woman hiding a wound. This legend, along with the fact that the woman of the house had a central role in dairy production, led to the idea that women could be involved in the theft of the farmers' 'profit'; old, widowed, unmarried or independent women were usually pinpointed as the main culprits.

These associations caused many people to believe hares were bad luck, and best avoided. A hare crossing one's path, particularly when the person was riding a horse, caused much distress. Still, the exact opposite superstition, claiming that carrying a rabbit's or hare's foot brought good luck, remained. There is no logic to be found in superstitions.

Despite this suspicious view of rabbits and their association with fertility and sexuality, Renaissance painters used the symbol of a white rabbit to convey a different meaning altogether: one of chastity and purity. It was generally believed that female rabbits could conceive and give birth without contact with the male of the species, and thus virginal white rabbits appear in biblical pictures of the Madonna and Child. The gentle timidity of rabbits also represented unquestioning faith in Christ's Holy Church in paintings such as Titian's *Madonna of the Rabbit* (1530).

The Hare

Witches constantly assume the form of a hare in order to gain entrance to a field where they can bewitch the cattle. A man once fired at a hare he met in the early morning and, having wounded it, followed the track of the blood till it disappeared within a cabin. On entering he found Nancy Molony, the greatest witch in the entire county, sitting by the fire, groaning and holding her side. And then the man knew that she had been out in the form of a hare, and he rejoiced over her discomfiture.

Or:

A tailor returning home very late at night from a wake, or it may be better to say very early in the morning, saw a hare sitting on the path before him, and not inclined to run away. He approached, with his stick raised to strike her. As he did so, he distinctly heard a voice saying, 'Don't kill it.' However, he struck the hare three times and each time heard the voice say, 'Don't kill it.' The last blow knocked the poor hare quite dead and immediately a great big weasel sat up and began to spit at him. This greatly frightened the tailor, who grabbed the hare and ran off as fast as he could. Seeing him look so pale and frightened, his wife asked the cause, upon which he told her the whole story. They both knew he had done wrong, and offended some powerful witch, who would be avenged.

However, they dug a grave for the hare and buried it, for they were afraid to eat it, and hoped that now perhaps the danger was over. However, the next day the man became suddenly speechless and died before the seventh day was over, without a word evermore passing his lips, and then all the neighbours knew that the witch-woman had taken her revenge.

26

THE BAT

(*Laltóg*)

FEARED AS CREATURES OF the night associated with death, sickness and witchcraft, bats were made famous as the familiars of vampires by the cinema. The learned folklorist Joseph Jacobs said, 'He that is neither one thing nor the other has no friends.' In Ireland if a bat was seen near the house it was taken as a sign of an impending death for a member of the household.

Revulsion towards them, however, is far from universal, and their quizzical faces have often inspired affection. Bats have often been identified in folk belief with the souls of the dead. As a result, in cultures that venerate ancestral spirits, bats are often considered sacred or beloved. When spirits are expected to pass on rather than return, bats appear as demons or, at best, souls unable to find peace.

A common bat seen in and around hedgerows at dusk is the pipistrelle bat. Their Irish name is *Laltog Fheascrach*, which means 'bat of the evening'.

A Tale of the Bat

Once upon a time, there was a big fight between the birds of the air and the animals with teeth that lived on the ground. The bat said to himself, 'I've got wings and I can fly so I think I'll be on the bird's side.'

Early on in the fight, the birds were losing so the bat crept away and hid under a log. He stayed there until the fighting stopped for a while. All the creatures wanted to go home for lunch. As the animals of the ground were passing by the bat's hiding place he slipped out and joined them.

'Hold on,' shouted one of the animals, looking closely at the bat. 'Aren't you one of those who fought against us? What are you doing here?'

'I?' said the bat, 'Oh no, not I. I'm one of you. I don't belong to the bird people. Just look in my mouth. Have you ever seen a bird with teeth like mine? No, I'm one of you people. My teeth are like yours.'

The animals of the ground looked at each other and nothing more was said and the bat stayed with them.

After lunch the animals and the birds went back to fighting again but this time the birds won and the bat sneaked off and hid under his log again. Soon it was dinner time and everyone went home for something to eat. As the birds flew by the bat crawled out from under his log and slipped in among them.

'What are you doing here?' said one of the birds. 'You are one of the animals of the ground, and we saw you fighting for them.'

'Who, me?' said the bat. 'Oh no, I'm one of you. I don't belong to the animals of the ground. Look at me; have you ever seen one of the animals of the ground with wings like mine? No, I'm one of you people; I'm like you.'

The birds looked at each other and nothing more was said and the bat stayed with them.

This went on day after day and the bat always joined the winning side when the fighting stopped but soon the animals and the birds said, 'This is silly, we shouldn't be fighting all the time'. So they decided to make friends. But what should they do about the bat?

The King of the Animals and the King of the Birds had a meeting to decide whether the bat belonged to the birds of the air or the animals of the ground. They decided that because the bat had teeth he was an animal but he also had wings so he must be a bird. However, because he was naughty, always joining the winning side, he could not be trusted so they said, 'Bat will fly like the birds but he will do so only at night when the animals are hunting. He will be alone and will never have any friends among those who fly or those who walk', and so it has been ever since.

Why the Bat Flies at Night

Once upon a time, long, long ago, when the world was first made it was never dark or cold. The sun shone bright and yellow all day and all the animals were lovely and warm and it was always light. At night time the moon shone bright and silvery; in fact, it was nearly as bright as day time. One day Mother Nature asked the bat if he could be trusted to go on a mysterious journey for her. She wanted the bat to carry a basket up to the moon as he had wings to fly and strong teeth to hold onto the handle of the basket. Inside the basket was all the black darkness in the world, but of course the bat didn't know this.

The bat flew off, carrying the basket between his teeth, but it soon became too heavy and he thought to himself, 'Oh dear, this basket is very heavy and I'm tired and hungry.'

So the bat flew down and went to find some food and have a little sleep. As he hung upside down in a nearby tree, some animals came walking along and saw the basket. They thought someone had lost it.

'That's a large basket' said one of them. 'I wonder if it's full of nice things to eat?'

'Let's open it and have a look,' said another.

Just as the animals were peeking under the lid, the bat came back. 'Hey, what are you doing to my basket?' shouted the bat.

The animals dropped the basket in shock. The bat tried to catch it but it was too late; it hit the ground and the lid fell off. All the darkness escaped.

Ever since that time the bat sleeps during the day and gets plenty of rest so he is ready to fly when the sun goes to bed and the moon comes out. When night time comes and it gets dark you will see him rushing about everywhere.

Do you know why?

Well, he is trying to catch all the pieces of the dark to put them back in the basket so he can take them to the moon.

That is the story of the bat.

27

THE WOOD MOUSE

(*Luch Fhéir/Luchóg*)

THE EARLIEST REMAINS OF wood mice in Ireland, date to the Stone Age, some 7,600 years ago. It is believed that more wood mice came to Ireland with humans at various times, giving a certain genetic variability. The wood mouse is a very important part of the Irish food web. Many Irish predators eat wood mice, including owls, kestrels, stoats, foxes, badgers, pine martens, and domestic cats. Wood mice are susceptible to pesticides, insecticides, and herbicides, and to the burning of straw. A decline in wood mice numbers can affect predator numbers, especially owls.

To hear a mouse squeaking anywhere near someone who is ill is a sign that the person will die and much of the abhorrence of mice (who are actually far cleaner creatures than generally imagined) probably stems from the old superstition that they are the souls of people who have been murdered. If they nibble anyone's clothing during the night, that person will suffer some misfortune, while no journey undertaken after seeing one is likely to be successful.

In Ireland boiled mice were given to infants to cure their incontinence and were also a cure for whooping cough.

Mice were used as a cure for baldness. A pot was filled with mice and left under the hearth for a year. You then spread the contents of the pot over your scalp. If for some reason you couldn't wait, then you moved the pot to the back of the hearth, lit a fire in front of it, then after six days you spread the contents onto the scalp.

The Mouse Trap

A mouse looked through the crack in the wall to see the farmer and his wife open a package.

'What food might this contain?' the mouse wondered.

He was devastated to discover it was a mousetrap. Retreating to the farmyard, the mouse began to shout out a warning, 'There's a mousetrap in the house! There's a mousetrap in the house!'

The chicken clucked and scratched, raised her head and said, 'Mr Mouse, I can tell this is a grave concern to you, but it's of no concern to me. I can't be bothered by it.'

The mouse turned to the pig and told him, 'There's a mousetrap in the house! There's a mousetrap in the house!'

The pig sympathised, but said, 'I am so very sorry, Mr Mouse, but there is nothing I can do about it, but be assured you're in my prayers. Oink oink.'

The mouse turned to the cow and said, 'There's a mousetrap in the house! There's a mousetrap in the house!'

The cow said, 'Mr Mouse, I'm sorry for you, but it's no skin off my nose. Moooove along.'

So, the mouse returned to the house, head down and dejected, to face the farmer's mousetrap alone.

That very night a sound was heard throughout the house – like the sound of a mousetrap catching its prey. The farmer's wife rushed to see what was caught. In the darkness, she didn't see it was a venomous snake whose tail the trap had caught. The snake bit the farmer's wife. The farmer rushed her to the hospital and she returned home with a fever.

Everyone knows you treat a fever with fresh chicken soup, so the farmer took his hatchet to the farmyard for the soup's main ingredient. However, his wife's sickness continued, so friends and neighbours came to sit with her around the clock.

To feed them, the farmer butchered the pig. The farmer's wife didn't get better and eventually she died. The whole community came for her funeral; the farmer had the cow slaughtered to provide enough meat for all of them.

The mouse looked upon it all from his crack in the wall with great sadness.

So, the next time you hear someone is facing a problem and think it doesn't concern you, remember: when one of us is threatened, we are all at risk. We are all involved in this journey called life. We must keep an eye out for one another and make an extra effort to encourage one another. Each one of us is a vital thread in another person's tapestry.

The Optimistic Mouse

As a storyteller and folklorist, I've collected many true stories about people who have done amazing things because they didn't know they were not supposed to be able to do them. I've also heard stories of people who never really managed to accomplish anything simply because they were told they would never amount to much.

Belief, or the lack of it, can limit your true potential; your belief in yourself can and does determine what you can or can't do in this life. It's not your intelligence, your gender or your wealth. It's not your parents, your age, race or physical appearance. If you change your belief about what is possible for you, then your behaviour will change as well. When these things both change, then your results will change also and all sorts of wonderful things will begin to happen for you. So don't let others put you down; believe in yourself and your time will come. The following stories may illustrate my point.

Two mice lived in a house. Both of them were young and full of energy. Each day, they would run, jump and chase each other while playing. Though they were equally strong, there was a difference: one mouse was optimistic and always lived in hope, while the other was pessimistic and lived in despair.

One day, while playing, both mice fell into a pot of milk. They swam around and tried to climb out, but, as there was no solid support under their feet, it was impossible for the mice to climb out and escape from the pot.

After some struggle, the pessimistic mouse said to itself, 'It is impossible to climb out. I have the strength but I can't swim very long. I'm already tired.' Soon the poor mouse became so tired he couldn't swim any longer. He gave up his struggle and sank down to the bottom of the pot, where he quickly drowned.

However, the optimistic mouse kept on struggling, saying to itself, 'I know it's difficult but if I believe in myself and keep swimming maybe some miracle will occur. If I try a little longer, something good might happen. If I keep trying then maybe I'll get out of here.'

Hoping for a miracle to happen, the second mouse went on swimming. His constant leg movements churned the milk and turned it into a huge heap of butter. Soon the mouse was able to climb up the heap of butter and hop out of the pot.

Positive thinking had saved the life of the mouse. So you see nothing is impossible as long as you don't give up.

The Mouse Who Believed in Himself

One day a group of mice were playing in a jungle when two of them fell into a pit full of water. The two mice didn't know how to swim, so they began to jump in an attempt to get out of the water and back on the bank. All the other young mice gathered around the pit to watch what was happening. On seeing the two mice jumping for their lives, some of the mice started clapping and shouting encouragement, hoping that the two mice would escape from the water.

However, some of the other mice started shouting, 'Hey, you fools, you'll never get out. The pit is very deep. Both of you are going to die soon.'

The two mice ignored the comments, and tried to jump up out of the pit. The naughty mice kept shouting, telling them to stop trying. Finally, one of the mice took its head out of water to hear what the other mice were saying. On hearing the comments, he got discouraged and gave up. He sank further into the water and, in no time, died.

The other mouse kept jumping as hard as he could. The crowd of mice kept telling him to stop trying, as it was futile. But the mouse jumped even harder and finally made it out. When the mouse came out, the other mice wondered how he had survived. Why did he keep jumping, despite the discouragement of the naughty mice? To their surprise they found that the second mouse was deaf and couldn't hear the negative comments.

When the naughty mice were clapping and shouting at the two mice, the second mouse thought that they were encouraging him to try harder to save himself. It was the positive belief in himself that saved his life.

28

THE RAT

(Francach)

MICE AND RATS WERE often depicted as the same animal in Irish folklore. They were believed to carry away the human soul after death or while the person was dreaming. Some people even believed that the soul left the body at night and turned into a rat or a mouse. If, for some reason, the soul did not return to the body then the person would die and that is why it was considered bad luck to wake a person who was sleep-walking. It was once believed that witches could turn themselves into rats or mice. One sad belief was that stillborn children took on the form of white mice or rats.

The Irish name, *Francach*, derives from the belief that the rat originally came here from France during the Anglo-Norman invasion. It is also known in ancient Ireland as *Luch* (the same word for mouse), although to distinguish them they were also called *Luch mór* (big mouse) while the mouse was *Luch beag* (small mouse). You could say it was the original invasive species, as is witnessed from the way it has spread across the world.

Rats are known as relentless survivalists that can adapt to many conditions. Their ability to breed and overrun a place, along with their association with disease, has made them almost universally reviled. Certainly a few enthusiasts enjoy the charms of these clever and prolific mammals, but most people cringe in their presence. Fear of rats has been a longstanding attitude throughout history. As they were hated and loathed so much, it is not surprising that most of the folklore concerning rats concerns different ways to get rid of them.

Since ancient times rats have been associated with the souls of people. Their supernatural character caused them to be regarded as ominous creatures that sometimes had foreknowledge of disaster. This is most frequently illustrated by reports of rats abandoning ships before putting to sea. When this happens, sailor superstition holds that the ship is doomed.

The dread of rats is not limited to seafaring folk. Rats are often the creatures in legends that act as agents of vengeance for murdered souls. A very gruesome story from Germany tells of how the Bishop Hatto of Mayence locked starving people in a barn during a famine in AD 970 and set the building on fire to reduce the number of hungry people in the region. There is no historical record to confirm this horrible story and there is no evidence of the supposed army of rats that hunted down the bishop and killed him, but it makes a good story.

Gaelic poets were said to be able to banish or kill rats with the power of their verse. Their power was even mentioned by Shakespeare in *As You Like It*. It was even believed that you could banish them by writing them a letter.

Rat superstitions:

- A great increase in the number of rats foretells a war. In County Wexford rats ran through all the houses in Kilmore before the war of 1641. They had not been seen there before.
- If a rat gnaws your clothing, you will soon remove your furniture from that house.
- Drop a baby's tooth into a rat hole and the new tooth will be beautiful.
- If a rat finds a tooth that you have thrown away, you will get a rat tooth.
- If you see rats leaving a building, it will soon burn.
- It is the sign of good luck to have a rat jump out of a drawer that you have opened.
- Rats will not remain in a cellar where there is a mole.
- To drive away rats, singe the hair from one rat and turn it loose.
- A white rat seen in a coal mine is a sign that a cave-in is imminent.
- You should never mend any clothes that a rat has chewed, for it will bring you bad luck.

The famous tale of the Pied Piper of Hamelin is a great example of how music is supposedly able to charm rats. In 1284, the Pied Piper is said to have emptied the town of rats by playing his pipe.

There is a story that is told in the Christian tradition concerning the rat and the devil. The devil saw that Noah had built an ark and was not happy, as he was looking forward to the destruction of the human race. He created a rat and dropped it onto the ark, intending it to either gnaw a hole in the ark, causing it to sink, or eat all their stores and cause them to starve to death. God saw what the devil was up to and told Noah to throw his glove at the rat. The glove turned into the first domestic cat and it killed the rat, so ending the devil's plan.

Another rather gruesome story told concerns St Fina, who, after many years of illness, was disabled by paralysis. She decided to lie on a wooden board as a bed in order to increase her suffering and offer this as a penance, hoping this would bring her closer to her god. As she lay on the board in her cold, damp attic, unable to move, she was attacked by rats, which fed upon her body.

The beady eyes and scuttling gait of rats will likely maintain their unpopularity among people. They will continue to breed and cause problems for humans, particularly as we have now supplied them with lovely comfy homes due to this new craze of wooden decking in the garden, coupled with the creation of composting areas built by people who are untrained in the art. Add to this the now prevalent build-up of black plastic bags containing waste in our rural areas as people wait until they have enough to make a trip to the land fill viable (we are no longer allowed to burn or bury our waste) and we have created rat heaven.

29

THE STOAT

(Easóg)

THE STOAT (*MUSTAFA ERMINEA*) is a member of the family Mustelidae that includes weasels, ferrets, martens and otters. The stoat is interchangeable with the weasel in Irish folklore. The Irish name, *easóg*, refers to its eel-like shape (*eas* is the Irish for eel) and the way its body undulates when it runs.

Rarely encountered in the flesh, but common in country tales, stoat packs have long hunted the borderland between folklore and natural history. It was once believed that the stoat was a form of cat brought to our shores as a pet by the Anglo-Normans.

The stoat has been present in Ireland since before the Ice Age and possibly survived here through the Ice Age too. In fact, we have our very own sub-species, with a whiter belly, that is only found in Ireland and the Isle of Man.

The following tale illustrates the closeness of the stoat pack.

On a mild, sunny day in March, a man was walking down a country lane. It was a lovely warm day and partridges could be heard calling to each other in the long grass. There was a lovely blue sky and all was right with the world. All of a sudden a pack of small animals charged down the nearby bank and surrounded the man. They began jumping up at his legs, snapping and biting with their sharp little fangs. They seemed to him to be like little furry snakes with murderous red eyes. They had four short legs, little pointed heads, flattened ears and rat-like tails. Their bodies seemed to flow as they ran. The man started beating them off with his stick. He managed to knock five or six of them into the ditch, kicking at the remainder, which had their fangs entangled in his trousers. He was horrified to see that those he had knocked into the ditch were coming at him again. Even though he was a brave man, he wasn't willing to carry on the fight and took his chance to break free and run for his life. He later found out that the snake-like creatures were members of a notorious stoat pack that terrorised the area.

Many are familiar with the paralysis stoats can inflict on rabbits, even at some distance, without knowing quite how they do it. Well documented also is the stoat's whirling dervish-like dance that mesmerises other animals until it darts forward and seizes one. Slightly less explicable is the dance that witnesses have reported the stoat performing as if in triumph over its already dispatched prey: 'It ran round and round the dead bird,' wrote one, 'sometimes almost turning head over heels; then it would break away and race off into the bushes, then back out again.' Stranger still is the fact that stoats carry their dead – appearing soon after one of their kind has been killed to drag the corpse into a hiding place.

It is perhaps such behaviour, along with their almost preternatural speed and flexibility that has given stoats a slightly uncanny character. They are elusive, usually solitary animals; collectively, however, they can induce a feeling of menace.

No one is really sure why stoats occasionally form packs. The ability to hunt bigger prey is one obvious motive, yet as many stoat packs have been recorded in times of plenty – high summer for instance – as during hard winters. A female stoat hunting with her large brood of kits (usually between six and twelve), or an accidental meeting of two family groups, giving a false impression of an organised pack, has also been suggested.

In Irish mythology, stoats were viewed as if they had human-like abilities, as animals with families, which held rituals for their dead. Stoats were also supposed to hold the souls of infants who died before baptism

They were viewed as noxious animals prone to thieving and their saliva was said to be able to poison a grown man. They were even believed to understand human speech. So greet them politely or suffer the consequences. It was believed that if you killed a stoat, its family would return and spit in the milk churn to poison it.

To encounter a stoat when setting out for a journey was considered bad luck, but one could avert this by greeting the stoat as a neighbour.

A purse or wallet made from the skin of a stoat was believed to bring great fortune for it would never be empty and the skin of a stoat was said to cure rat bites.

If a woman cut off the testicles of a male stoat, stitched them into a wee bag and wore it round her neck, it was thought to act as a form of contraception. (Well, it would certainly put me off.)

Stoats are totally protected in Ireland. If stoats are proving a problem, by killing chicks or other domestic animals, you must solve the problem by using good fencing; it is illegal to kill a stoat.

30

THE BUTTERFLY AND THE MOTH

(Féileacán)

FEW PEOPLE KNOW HOW the butterfly got its name. It was due to a witch who changed her shape into this insect. She then flew to the dairy, and stole milk, cheese and, of course, butter!

The transformation of a caterpillar into a butterfly seems to provide the ultimate model for our ideas of death, burial, and resurrection. This imagery is still implicit in Christianity when people speak of being 'born again'. The chrysalis of a butterfly may have even inspired the splendour of many coffins from antiquity. Many cocoons are very finely woven, with some threads that are golden or silver in colour. The Greek word '*psyche*' means soul, but it can also designate a butterfly or moth. The Latin word '*anima*' has the same dual meaning.

The custom of scattering flowers at funerals is very ancient. The flowers attract butterflies, which appear to have emerged from a corpse.

A butterfly or moth will hover for a time in one place or fly in a fleeting, hesitant manner, suggesting a soul that is reluctant to move on to the next world. An old Irish saying is that 'Butterflies are souls of the dead waiting to pass through Purgatory'. In certain areas of Ireland, people believe that a white butterfly or moth is a soul on its way to paradise. If the wings are spotted, the soul must pay for its sins in purgatory but a pure soul will be all white. It other areas it was believed that white butterflies hold the souls of dead children and up to the 1600s it was against common law in Ireland to kill a white butterfly. The red admiral butterfly, however, was thought to be the devil and was persecuted.

As butterflies were considered souls, they were also believed to have the ability to cross into the Otherworld and were a symbol of transformation and creation. According to people in certain areas of Mexico, monarch butterflies carry the spirits of dead ancestors back to visit our world. They arrive each year on (or near) the Day of the Dead (2 November) to visit and to take the souls of the newly departed away with them.

'For Christians, the butterfly's three steps of metamorphosis – as caterpillar, pupa and then winged insect – are reminiscent of spiritual transformation.'

A traditional Irish blessing was as follows: 'May the wings of the butterfly kiss the sun and find your shoulder to light upon. To bring you luck, happiness and riches today and beyond.'

If the first butterfly you see in the year is white, you will have good luck all year and three butterflies together mean a child will soon be born. However, a white moth inside the house or trying to enter the house means death, but a brown moth means an important letter is coming. A big black moth in the house means a deceased one is visiting, reincarnated in that moth.

According to superstition, the death's-head hawk moth, with its skull and crossbones markings and loud squeak, was a harbinger of death, war and disease. The moth uses its tough proboscis to crack through beehives and suck out honey and in some parts of Ireland is known as a bee robber.

If anyone desires a wish to come true, they must first capture a butterfly and whisper that wish to it. Since a butterfly can make no sound, the butterfly can not reveal the wish to anyone but the Great Spirit who hears and sees all. In gratitude for giving the beautiful butterfly its freedom, the Great Spirit always grants the wish. So, according to legend, by making a wish and giving the butterfly its freedom, the wish will be taken to the heavens and will be granted.

Native Americans embroidered butterflies onto their children's caps to bring sweet dreams.

The Priest's Soul: A Story about the First Butterfly

Once upon a time, far back in the mists of time, Ireland was known as the land of saints and scholars. Kings and queens would send their sons here to be educated. At that time there was a poor young boy who was known to everyone for his intelligence and although his parents were but lowly labourers he came to the attention of one of the priests who taught those of wealth that were sent to him.

This priest was the cleverest priest in Ireland. However, he had grown very vain and proud. He had forgotten his own lowly beginnings and had even forgotten his god, whom his faith had taught him was the one who had made him what he was. His pride in winning every argument led him to believe that he could prove there was no purgatory, no hell, indeed no heaven, and so, logically, there was no god and no soul. In fact, we were no better than the beast of the field and when we died there was no rebirth or resurrection.

'Who ever saw a soul?' he would say. 'If you can show me one, only then will I believe.'

No one had an answer for that; and at last they all came to believe that as there was no other world, you might as well do as you liked in this one; the priest set the example, by taking a beautiful young girl as his wife. However, as no priest or bishop in the whole of Ireland could be got to marry them, he read the service himself. Well, of course, it was a great scandal, but no one dared to say a word because he had all the kings' sons on his side and, as they were heavily armed, they'd have slaughtered anyone who tried to prevent the wicked goings-on.

One night an angel appeared to the priest just as he was going to bed. He told the priest that he had twenty-four hours to live.

'Why? What have I done?' cried the priest,

The angel just looked at him, as much as to say, 'Are you joking?'

'Give me more time,' said the priest, but the angel refused.

'Arragh, go on, have pity on my poor soul,' said the priest.

'But you have no soul. Isn't that what you've been teaching others?' replied the angel.

'I have a soul; I can feel it fluttering in my chest ever since you appeared. I was just being a fool before,' answered the priest.

'Well, you got that right,' said the angel. 'What good was all your learning when you forgot your soul?'

'If I am to die, will I go to heaven?' asked the priest hopefully,

'No, didn't you deny heaven even existed?' replied the angel.

'Well, how about purgatory then?'

'No, you denied that as well, so it's straight to hell for you, my boy,' said the angel.

'Ah, now, hang on a minute, didn't I also deny there was a hell? So you can't send me there either.'

The angel was a little puzzled.

'Well,' said the angel, after a little thought, 'I'll tell you what I can do for you. You may either live here on earth for another hundred years, enjoying every pleasure, and then be cast into Hell forever or you may die in twenty-four hours in the most horrible torments and pass through to purgatory, there to remain till the Day of Judgement. However, seeing as you've done such a good job convincing everyone that God doesn't exist, you must find one person that believes, and through their belief mercy will be given to you and your soul will be saved.'

The priest just took a few seconds to make up his mind. 'I will have death in the twenty-four hours,' he said, 'so that my soul may be saved at last.' So the angel gave him directions as to what he was to do and left him.

Immediately, the priest entered the large room where all his scholars and the kings' sons were seated. The priest asked them, 'Have men souls?'

They answered, 'We used to think so but you convinced us otherwise.'

The priest replied, 'I taught you a lie, now I believe there is a god and we do have an immortal soul.'

Of course they all laughed at him for they thought this was just a trick to start another argument. 'Prove it,' they said.

Next he went to his wife, but she also laughed at him and walked away, shaking her head. He ran from the house and asked every person he met if they believed, but they all laughed at him. Just as despair seemed to rise up all around him, a little boy came by.

'God bless and save you,' said the child.

The priest jumped up, 'Do you believe in God, child?'

'Of course, I've travelled the length of Ireland to learn about him. Will you direct me to the best place to go to learn more?' answered the child.

'The best place and the best teacher is here,' said the priest and pointed to himself.

When the priest told the boy his name, he said, 'Aren't you the priest who does not believe in a soul because it cannot be seen?

'I was,' replied the priest.

'Well, that's stupid for I can tell you that the soul does exist,' said the boy.

'How can you be so sure?' the priest inquired,

'I would say to you show me life if you believe you have life,' replied the boy.

'But that's impossible; life cannot be seen for it is invisible,' said the priest,

The boy replied, 'So is the soul.'

When the priest heard him speak these words, he fell down on his knees before him; now he knew his soul would go to heaven for he had found one who believed. He told the child his whole story.

The priest's time on this earth was quickly coming to an end; the twenty-four hours given to him by the angel would soon run out so he said to the young boy, 'Wait with me until you see death upon my face, then watch as my soul ascends into heaven. When you see this happen, run and tell everyone you see that man has an immortal soul and heaven does exist.'

The boy waited with the priest and held his hand until death came to claim his soul. As the priest breathed his last, the child saw a beautiful living creature with four snow-white wings rise up from the middle of the priest's chest and flutter around his head. He ran and brought back some of those that he met and when they saw it they all knew it was the soul of the priest and they watched in wonder as it passed from sight and disappeared into the clouds.

It is said that this was the first butterfly to be seen in Ireland and Irish folklore came to embrace the belief that the butterfly is the soul of one who has passed off this mortal coil and is just waiting for the moment the doors of heaven open so they may pass through into eternal peace. You see, sometimes it's enough to have the simple belief of a child.

The White Butterfly

An old man named Michael lived in a little house behind the cemetery out on the West Road near Westport in County Mayo. He was extremely friendly and liked by his neighbours, though most of them considered him to be a little quaint. Apparently this was because he had never married or even kept the company of women. One summer day he became very ill, so ill, in fact, that he sent for his sister-in-law and her son. They both came and did all they could to bring him comfort during his last hours. While they watched, Michael fell asleep; however, he had no sooner done so than a large white butterfly flew into the room and rested on the old man's pillow. His nephew tried to drive it away through an open window but it came back three times – it seemed that it didn't want to leave Michael.

At last Michael's nephew chased it out into the garden, through the gate and into the cemetery beyond, where it lingered over a woman's grave and then mysteriously disappeared. On examining the grave the young man found the name 'Mary' written upon it, together with an inscription telling how Mary had died when she was just eighteen. Though the gravestone was covered with moss and must have been erected fifty years previously, the nephew saw that it was surrounded with flowers, and that there was a little water jug that had been recently filled.

When the young man returned to the house, he found that Michael had passed away and he returned to his mother and told her what he had seen in the cemetery. 'Mary?' murmured his mother. 'When your uncle was young, he was betrothed to Mary. She died of consumption shortly before her wedding day. When Mary left this world, your uncle resolved never to marry and to live ever near her grave. For all these years, he has remained faithful to his vow and kept in his heart all the sweet memories of his one and only love. Every day Michael went to the cemetery, whether the air was fragrant with summer breeze or thick with falling snow. Every day he went to her grave and prayed for her happiness. He kept it weeded and set flowers there. When Michael was dying and he could no longer perform his loving task, Mary came for him. That white butterfly was her sweet and loving soul.'

31

THE LADYBIRD

(Bóín Dé)

HOW DID THE LADYBIRD get its name? Well, there are a number of different explanations, depending on which story you choose to believe. One says that in Europe of the Middle Ages, swarms of insects were destroying the crops and people did not know what to do. They decided to pray to the Virgin Mary for help. Shortly afterwards, the ladybirds arrived and ate all the insects that had been feeding on the crops. The people called these beautiful insects Our Lady's beetles and over time this was shortened to Lady beetles. The red wings of the ladybird represent the Virgin Mary's cloak, the black spots symbolise both her joys and sorrows.

There are a number of superstitions surrounding the ladybird. It is believed that they bring good luck and they were once considered a symbol of protection. If you hold a ladybird while making a wish, then the direction the ladybird flies in will tell you the direction the answer to your wish will come from.

However, if you harm or kill one, then you will suffer bad luck. It seems surprising therefore that it was believed that ladybirds ground up into a powder and taken will cure toothache, measles, stomach complaints, and crying babies.

The arrival of ladybirds foretells the onset of good weather and, if they were seven-spotted ladybirds, there will be a good harvest. However, more than seven spots indicate that a famine could be expected.

There was an old rhyme that children would recite, all but forgotten now. It is suggested that it originated from the practice of burning the fields in order to prepare them for replanting. It goes something like this:

> Ladybird, ladybird, fly away home,
> Your house is on fire, your children are gone.
> All but one and her name is Ann
> And she has crept under the frying pan.

Farmers recited the rhyme whilst holding a ladybird, which was then blown off the hand. Many such poems were taught to children as a way of encouraging them to look after the ladybird and set it free as it was a beneficial insect for the rural Irish.

32

THE BUMBLEBEE

(Bumbóg)

BUFF-TAILED BUMBLEBEE NESTS CAN be found in the hedgerows and the bees may be seen coming and going through a hole in the ground. The nest itself will be hard to see as bees are very private individuals, but if you listen carefully you may hear them buzzing away quite happily. Sometimes the queen may decide to occupy an old abandoned mouse nest as these are usually warm and well insulated. She may also nest underneath sheds, decking, in compost bags, in hedge clippings or even in attics or under floorboards. You could move a nest if it was causing you problems but it might not fully recover. Therefore, you would be better off leaving it alone if it is doing you no harm. Like all bumblebees, they need to be greatly provoked before they sting.

As bees are becoming victim to an ever-changing world that threatens their habitat, you can do your bit to help them survive. Plant suitable flowers in your garden, window boxes, containers or even along the hedgerow. Provide a nest box; these are now becoming increasingly available in good garden centres or you could build your own (they are very easy to make and instructions can be found on the internet). Remember: they are a gardener's friend and we need bees to pollinate our plants.

There is a superstition that if a bumblebee buzzes at the window it is a sign of a coming visitor. If it has a red tail, the visitor will be a man and if the tail is white the visitor will be a lady.

Irish folklore tells us how easily the bees take offence which can cause them to cease producing honey, desert their hives and die. You must treat bees as you would a member of your own family. They must be told all the news, in particular births, deaths and marriages. 'Telling the Bees' was extremely important, whether it was good news or bad or just everyday gossip. Bad news was given before sunrise of the following day for all to be well. You had to tell the bees about a death in the family or the bees would die too. In the event of a death, their hive had to be adorned with a black cloth or ribbon and they had to be given their share of the funeral food. You could even formally invite the bees to attend the funeral or you could turn the beehives round as the coffin was carried out of the house and past the hives. In ancient European folklore, bees were regarded as messengers of the gods and so the custom of 'Telling the Bees' may be a throwback to the idea of keeping the gods informed of human affairs.

Another belief was that if the bees heard you quarrelling or swearing, they would leave so you had to talk to them in a gentle manner. You might then hear them gently hum in contentment and they would stay with you. It was said they could not tolerate the presence of a woman of loose morals or one that was menstruating, but would sting her and drive her away (this sounds like a Christian influence). You must never buy bees with normal money, only with gold coin, although you may obtain them as a gift, loan or barter. It was also believed that if a single bee entered your house, it was a sign of good luck on the way, usually in the form of wealth.

When bees swarmed, the women and children of the household had to follow them, making a noise with pots and pans. This was supposed to make them settle or maybe it was really just to warn people to get out of the way? It was accepted that in these circumstances you could follow them onto someone else's land without being accused of trespassing. The law on bees (Brehon Law) was that bees taking nectar from plants growing on your neighbour's land were guilty of grazing trespass in the same way a cow or sheep would be if they were on your neighbour's land. They could even be accused of leaping trespass in the same way as poultry. The way this law was observed was that a beekeeper was allowed three years of freedom, during which time the bees were allowed free reign; on the fourth year the first swarm to issue from the hive had to be given to your neighbour as payment. On the following years, other swarms were given in turn to other neighbours; in this way everyone was happy. From all accounts it seemed to work.

Another issue for which the Bechbretha (law governing bees) was enacted was in the event of stings. As long as you swore you had not retaliated by killing the bee, you would be entitled to a meal of honey from the beekeeper. However, if the unfortunate person died from a sting, then two hives had to be paid in compensation to their family.

It was a bad omen if a swarm settled on a dead branch for it meant death for someone in the beekeeper's family or for the person who witnessed the swarm settling. Popular folklore also suggested that bee stings aid in the relief of arthritis and rheumatism in much the same way as nettle stings and recently bee venom has been revived as a possible treatment for multiple sclerosis.

In Celtic myth, bees were regarded as beings of great wisdom and as spirit messengers between worlds. Honey was treated as a magical substance and used in many rituals. It was made into mead and was considered to have prophetic powers and it may have been why it was called 'nectar of the gods'. The rivers that lead to the summer lands are said to be rivers of mead.

St Modomnoc O'Neil and the Bees

In Irish folklore there is a story concerning a young man who wanted to be a priest. His name was Modomnoc and he is often referred to as the Patron Saint of Bees. He left Ireland and went to Wales, where he joined a Menevia monastery, and it was there that he began his religious education under the tutelage of a great teacher known as David, later to become St David. In common with all monasteries, the workload was divided among those who resided in the monastery.

Modomnoc was given responsibility for the bees, a job which he relished. He cared for them, keeping them in straw skeps (portable beehives) in a sheltered corner of the garden and planted a variety of flowers that he knew would please the bees. This suited all the other monks as they all loved honey but very few of them liked to work with bees. Whenever the bees swarmed, Modomnoc captured the swarm and very gently placed the swarm into a new skep. When bees swarm, it is their way of relocating with the old queen bee because a new queen in the hive/skep has taken over the colony. Usually half the colony will follow the old queen to a new location. Swarming is the natural way for honeybees to reproduce a new colony and normally takes place in early spring.

Modomnoc talked to his bees as he worked among them, telling them all the news, and they were seen buzzing around his head as though they were listening to every word. The bees repaid Modomnoc's kindness by producing so much honey that he had to ask other monks to help him carry it into the monastery kitchen. It was due to his kind and caring treatment of the bees that the monks never ran out of honey. They were able to use it in a variety of ways, from making cakes and bread and gallons of mead, their favourite drink.

Modomnoc thanked his god for blessing him with a love for his bees and in the evening the other monks would see him walking among the skeps, talking to the bees that would fly around him as though they had come out to meet him. However, the other monks kept well away from Modomnoc's area of the garden as they had no wish to be stung, although no bee was ever known to sting Modomnoc.

Eventually the time came for Modomnoc to leave; his studies completed, he wished to return to Ireland to begin teaching the word of God to his countrymen. Although he was happy and excited at the prospect of returning home, he also felt a little sadness for he knew that he would have to leave his beloved bees behind. On the day of his departure, he said goodbye to the abbot and his fellow monks. He then sadly walked down to his corner of the garden to say farewell to his friends the bees. Hive after hive of bees came out to meet him in their thousands, buzzing and flying around him in excitement. Abbot David and the other monks stood at a safe distance and watched the spectacle in silence. One monk turned to the abbot and quietly said, 'You'd think that the bees know he's leaving.'

Modomnoc turned away from the garden and sadly made his way down to the seashore, where he boarded the ship that would take him home to Ireland. Modomnoc stood on deck and watched as the coast of Wales receded into the distance. When the ship was about 3 miles from the shore, Modomnoc saw what appeared to be a black cloud approaching their ship. He watched as it approached and suddenly, to his amazement, he realised what it was. It was a swarm of bees coming nearer and nearer until finally it settled on the side of the ship near where he stood. The swarm was huge; it looked as though every single bee from all the monastery hives had followed him. Modomnoc was not pleased and said to the bees, 'How foolish of you to follow me. You belong to the monastery. How are my brother monks suppose to manage with no honey for their baking or making mead? Go home this instant.'

However, if the bees understood him, they chose to completely ignore him and settled down with a low buzzing that sounded a little like they were snoring and stayed exactly where they were. The sailors who manned the ship were not very happy with this at all as they were scared of the bees and the captain demanded that Modomnoc do something before there was a mutiny on board. Modomnoc asked the captain to turn the ship round and return to Wales. It was too far for the bees to fly back as they were very tired and he did not want his little friends to be harmed; after all, they were only doing what they believed was the right thing to do. When the sailors turned back to Wales, the wind was blowing towards Ireland so they had to drop the sail and row back to the shore. They were furious but said nothing to Modomnoc as they were afraid of what the bees might do if they felt he was being threatened.

When the abbot saw that Modomnoc had returned, he was extremely surprised and asked for an explanation. Modomnoc told him all that had happened since he had left and the refusal of the bees to return of their own accord. The abbot listened with interest and then suggested that Modomnoc stay the night in his old room and try again in the morning. However, this time he advised him to say nothing to the bees and just leave quietly before they knew what was happening.

Next morning, the ship was once again ready to leave and this time Modomnoc did what the abbot had suggested. He left without any fuss or tearful goodbyes and sailed away into the distance. However, once again, as he was stood on the deck looking back to the coast of Wales, he saw a black cloud rise up from the Welsh coast and he knew what that meant. The captain ordered the ship to turn around immediately. Modomnoc went ashore and walked back to the monastery to ask the abbot for his advice.

'What am I to do? I must return home but the bees won't let me leave without them. I can't let them come with me because then you will have nothing left. They are far too valuable to the monastery.'

The abbot listened to Modomnoc and then made his decision.

'Modomnoc, I give you the bees. Take them with my blessing for they will not live without you. God will provide and we will get other bees for the monastery.'

The abbot accompanied Modomnoc back down to the shore and spoke to the sailors. 'If the bees follow Modomnoc for the third time, take them to Ireland with my blessing.'

The sailors were not happy with this but the abbot assured them that the bees would give them no trouble as long as Modomnoc was on board the ship. This seemed to satisfy the crew and for the third time the ship set sail for Ireland. Modomnoc prayed that the bees would have the sense to stay in their pretty little garden in the monastery. When they were roughly 3 miles from the Welsh coast, Modomnoc saw the black cloud rise up once more, but this time the boat did not turn back. Resigning himself to the will of God and the persistence of the bees, Modomnoc persuaded the swarm to settle in a sheltered corner of the ship and there they remained until they reached the shore of Ireland.

Modomnoc eventually set up his church at Bremore, near Balbriggan in County Dublin. He established a little garden similar to the monastery garden in Wales and the bees settled into their new home. The place is still known as 'The Church of the Beekeeper'. St Modomnoc died around 550 AD and his saint's day is celebrated on 13 February.

33

THE DEVIL'S COACH HORSE BEETLE

(Dubh Dael)

THIS BEETLE HAS BEEN associated with the Devil since the Middle Ages, hence its common name. It is found in damp conditions, such as under hedgerows and in woodland, and feeds on carrion and decaying matter. However, it may wander into your house and give you a bit of a fright. If approached, it raises its tail in a threatening manner as if to sting and lifts its head to show its open claws. Although harmless, this creature is hideous to look at and has long been a symbol of corruption. It was believed that it had the power to kill on sight and that it would eat sinners. When the beetle raised its tail, it was thought to be casting a curse.

In Ireland there is a strange legend that tells of the devil's coach horse and Jesus. The day before Jesus was betrayed, he was walking past a field where the local people were sowing corn. As Jesus passed by, he blessed the work and the corn crop grew extremely quickly. The amazed people declared it to be truly a miracle. The following day the Jews and soldiers who were searching for Jesus arrived at the field and asked the people if they had seen him. They answered that yes, they had seen him, but it was when the corn was being sown. The soldiers looked at the field of fully grown corn and said that it must have been quite a while ago and they turned to go back the way they had come. However, the Devil, taking the shape of the devil's coach horse, stuck his head up in the air and shouted, 'Yesterday, he was here yesterday', and with his upturned tail he indicated the way that Jesus had gone and so the enemies of Jesus were set upon his track. It is for this reason that it has been hated by all and many believe the Devil's coach horse must be killed whenever it is seen.

Another story tells us that the devil's coach horse gained the hatred of mankind when it was said to have eaten the core of the apple discarded by Eve in the Garden of Eden. To this day there is a strong smell of apples when the beetle is crushed. In Ireland it was suggested that you should crush it, preferably with your bare foot, for you would then be spared a day, hour or week in Purgatory. It was also believed in counties Cavan, Louth and Meath that anyone killing a devil's coach horse would be forgiven seven sins. However, if they killed one on a Friday then the sins of the whole week would be forgiven. In other countries the devil's coach horse is never crushed; instead it is burned.

Other names include Devil's Footman, Devil's coachman, Devil's steed, and coffin cutter. In Ireland the beetle is known as *darbhadal* (literally Devil's beast) and it is said that the Devil assumes the form of this beetle to eat sinners. As with many supposed bringers of ill luck, superstition holds that people can turn the creature's powers to their own advantage by acquiring power over others by cursing them. This was done by pointing the beetle with its tail upraised in their direction

It is said that the Grim Reaper used to enclose the body of a Devil's coach horse beetle in the handle of his scythe to improve its cutting skill. The origins of these beliefs can perhaps be explained by the beetle's threatening appearance, and its habit of eating carrion.

34

THE GARDEN SNAIL

(Seilide Gairdín)

WE ALL HAVE THEM in the garden; they are a pain in the neck, eating your lettuce and making holes in the cabbage. However, live snails are now being hailed as the new fountain of youth, giving you young, beautiful, smooth skin as they crawl across your face as part of a snail facial massage that was launched in Tokyo but is taking off across Europe.

The new craze is called the Celebrity Escargot Course. It lasts sixty minutes and people are willing to pay huge money for the privilege. You have to lie down and then snails are placed on your face; as they slide happily along, they leave behind a trail of mucus slime and this is the key. The slime is said to be full of beauty boosting proteins and goodies that help skin retain moisture, remove inflammation and dead skin. It has even been suggested that the snail facial may help to heal damaged skin. Facial masks containing creams made with an infusion of snail mucus have also been produced for clients to use at home.

Snails also feature in Irish folk medicine, particularly for curing warts in what is called a 'wasting cure'. The warts are rubbed with a snail (some would suggest a black snail) and the snail is then impaled on a thorn tree (hawthorn/blackthorn). As the snail dries up, withers and wastes away, the warts also disappear. Some examples suggest that a slug will work equally as well.

The slime produced by slugs/snails has been used in many cultures throughout time for treating a variety of minor wounds and skin ailments.

I have heard of other rather disgusting cures for curing coughs with snail juice. The snails are gathered early in the morning when the dew is still upon them. The shells are removed and the snail is placed in a jar with some sugar. The resulting concoction is then left to ferment and turn into a 'juice', which is administered to the sufferer. However, I would never suggest that anyone consumes snails or slugs as they can also carry diseases from rats. The slugs/snails become infected by consuming the infected faeces of rats.

Another 'cure' relates to earache. It was suggested that if you pricked a snail/slug with a sharp thorn it would release 'foam juice'. You would then drop the whole thing, foam and all, into the affected ear in order to 'cure' the earache.

35

THE SPIDER

(An Damhán Alla)

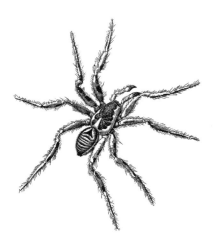

THERE ARE MANY SPIDER superstitions in Irish folklore.
Seeing a spider run down a web in the afternoon means you'll take
a trip. Spiders are a sign of St Michael. If you kill a spider you will
invoke bad weather. Never kill a spider in the afternoon or evening,
but always kill the spider unlucky enough to show himself early in
the morning, for the old French proverb says: 'A spider seen in the
morning is a sign of grief; a spider seen at noon, of joy; a spider
seen in the evening, of hope.' Personally, I would never kill a spider
no matter what time of day or night it was.

Cobwebs have been used to stop bleeding when de-horning cattle. They were also used in wound care in ancient Ireland. Charles Stuart Parnell crushed his hand in machinery at his Arklow quarries and an old servant dressed the injured fingers with cobwebs from the cellar walls.

Ireland has now become the home for a species of spider that is thought to have originated in the Canary Islands and Madeira. They were first recorded here in the 1870s; however, it has been suggested that they may have been on our shores as early as the 1480s. This period was known as the Age of Discovery, when trading ships travelled the world, bringing back cargos from strange and exotic lands. It is thought that these ships transported various new life forms hidden in their holds.

All spiders have the potential to bite; all have venomous fangs with which they subdue their prey or defend themselves. However, the species known as false widows have venom that can have a bigger effect upon humans. There are two species. The *Steatoda grossa*, the smaller of the two, was first spotted in Southern Ireland in the 1870s where it remained until the late 1900s, when it began to spread further north. In the 1990s, the larger *Steatoda noblis* appeared and began to spread all over the east coast and the midlands, where it has now become a common sight.

They are called false widows because they are almost identical to the true black widow spiders, the *Latrodectids*, but these spiders are not generally found living wild in Ireland, Britain or Scandinavia. Most spiders that fall under the description of false widow are not harmful to humans, but the two species of *Steatoda* are mildly venomous. They are not aggressive and mostly live outside among hedgerows, etc. They may enter sheds or even some old houses but generally like to keep to themselves and will not bother you if you don't bother them.

The venom of false widows is similar to and has roughly the same effect as wasp venom and the sting, though a little painful, is usually harmless and can be treated by rubbing it with a dock leaf or applying a little ordinary baking soda. However, all stings should be checked out as any sting could cause allergic reactions or symptoms indicating more serious ailments. The false widow spider is about the size of a twenty-cent coin, with a dark shiny body, pale markings, and a cream band on its abdomen and is thought to be spreading; one reason suggested for this is climate change.

Spiders and Tinsel

There was a time when animals were allowed into the house at Christmas, even the milk cow and the family pig. This was said to be because Jesus was born in a stable, amongst the animals. However, housewives kept the spiders out because, as everyone knows, spiders are a bit messy, leaving cobwebs all over the place. (It appears no one noticed the cowpats, pig droppings, etc.)

When Santa arrived on Christmas Eve, the spiders were very upset at being excluded and appealed to him for his help. Santa let them in so they could see the Christmas tree and they became so excited that they began to spin webs all over it. Santa decided that the webs looked so pretty as they glistened in the moonlight and he turned them into tinsel. The housewives were delighted and from that day onwards spiders have lived with humans.

And that is the story of how we came to have tinsel upon the Christmas tree.

36

THE COMMON NEWT AND THE LIZARD

(An Niút)

THE COMMON NEWT, THE lizard, and a multitude of large caterpillars were all looked upon by the Irish peasantry as 'worms'. They were also looked upon as being extremely dangerous to both man and beast and were killed whenever they were seen at large. The superstition surrounding these unfortunate creatures would not have helped as they were said to crawl down people's throats while they slept, which would result in that person dying a slow and painful death. Children were told that if they slept with their mouths open then 'worms' would crawl down their throats. These 'worms' included caterpillars and frogs. It is thought that the finding of flukes and parasites in sheep and cattle reinforced this belief.

The common newt, also known as the *Alp Luachra*, was believed to have the power to heal burns. It was once believed that if a person licked the back or belly of the *Alp Luachra* nine times then it would impart this power to the tongue of that person. Their saliva would then have the power to heal a burn.

The Alp Luachra

In Irish folklore the *Alp Luachra* was an evil parasitic creature that appeared as a small green newt or lizard. It would climb down the throat of anyone who was unfortunate enough to fall asleep by the side of a stream. Once this creature of the fairy realm entered the person's stomach, it would consume whatever food it could find there. It was believed that the *Alp Luachra* would remain in the stomach and might even invite others to join it until the person died of starvation. The *Alp Luachra* was also thought to have the power of invisibility, which enabled it to sit beside a person's plate and eat whatever food was placed upon it without being seen by those around the table.

Today I suppose the *Alp Luachra* would be described as a tapeworm. Like many other dark creatures of the fairy realm, the *Alp Luachra* was very selfish, thinking only of its own comforts and not caring about the human it fed off. However, they were not that clever and it was relatively easy to outsmart them. One story said that the way to rid yourself of an *Alp Luachra* was by eating a large quantity of salted meat. This would cause the *Alp Luachra* to become extremely thirsty and it would escape from within the human to search for water. There is an old story passed down in Connacht in the west of Ireland concerning the legend of the *Alp Luachra*.

The Legend of the Alp Lauchra

Once upon a time, there was a wealthy farmer in Connacht. He had plenty of land, cattle, a lovely wife and beautiful children. He was a very lucky man, healthy, strong and without a care in the world. However, his luck was about to change. It was the time of the harvest and he was watching his farmhands saving hay in one of the meadows near his house. The day was hot and as the sun bore down upon him he felt a mighty thirst. He reached down to where the farmhands had left a large jug of buttermilk and took a long cooling drink and then he lay down on a pile of freshly gathered hay and soon fell fast asleep.

He lay like that for about three or four hours. All the hay was gathered in and, having finished their work, the men went back to their own homes. When the farmer woke up, he was surprised at the late hour and, realising he must have been asleep for a good while, he stood up and headed back to his own house, which was nearby. As he walked through the fields, he felt a pain in his side but thought nothing of it other than that he must have been lying on a bit of a stone or something. Arriving back home, he sat down by the fireside and lit his pipe.

'Where were you? he men finished hours ago,' his daughter asked.

'It was so warm, I fell asleep on the grass where they were gathering hay,' he replied.

'Are you alright? You don't look too well.'

'I'm not sure. I have a queer feeling in my stomach. I've never felt anything like it before. I think I'll go for a lie down; maybe then I'll feel a bit better,' he replied.

He went to his bed, lay down, and fell fast asleep. He woke up later that night and went into the kitchen.

'You have been asleep a long time. What is wrong?' asked his wife.

'I don't know what it is. I just don't feel right,' said the husband.

He went over to the fireside, sat down in his chair and lit his pipe.

The following morning, the farmer, having slept late, which was extremely unusual for any farmer, sat by the fire where his daughter had a cake baking on the griddle. Seeing her father, she asked him, 'How are you feeling today, Daddy? Are you any better?'

'Well, I got a good night's sleep, but to be honest I'm feeling worse than I did last night. You won't believe this, but I think I have something inside me, running backwards and forwards,' replied her father.

'Arragh, you probably just picked up a bit of cold lying on that damp grass yesterday. If you're still no better this evening, I'll ask Mammy if I should get the doctor.'

That evening they sent for the doctor as the farmer seemed to be getting worse. For some reason the doctor was delayed and this caused the farmer to become extremely agitated and afraid because the pain had become so bad he actually thought he was dying.

At last the doctor arrived, went into the bedroom and asked the farmer what seemed to be the trouble and once again the farmer mentioned the fact that he felt as if there was something alive crawling around inside his stomach. The doctor gave him a full examination but could find nothing out of the ordinary. He listened to his chest but heard nothing, even when the farmer shouted, 'Now, did you hear that? Did you hear it moving?'

However, the doctor shook his head; he had heard nothing. After he had finished his examination, the doctor went out and spoke to the farmer's wife and daughter. He told them that he could find nothing physically wrong with the farmer but he thought that there must be some reason for the pain so he would send her some medicine the next day that should lower his temperature and help him get a good night's sleep. The doctor was as good as his word and the following day the medicine arrived and, having taken it, the farmer did indeed get a wonderful night's sleep. Unfortunately, when he woke up the following morning, he was worse than ever; the only difference was that he could not hear or feel the thing jumping around inside him.

His wife sent for the doctor again but he was unable to do anything more for the poor man other than leave him more medicines and return later that week to see if his condition had improved.

When he returned, the farmer was in a terrible state. The doctor was at a loss as to what was wrong and even refused to accept any more payment from the family as he felt he could do nothing to warrant it. The doctor said, 'I can find no reason for his sickness; all I can do is call in from time to time to check on him but I will take no money from you.'

The farmer's wife was very angry. She couldn't understand why, with all his training, the doctor was unable to do anything. She said to her daughter, 'That fellah is a complete eejit. Well, he won't be allowed into this house again. The next time we'll get the other doctor.'

The next time, true to her word, the farmer's wife sent for the other doctor. He turned out to be just as clueless as the first doctor and could do nothing to help her husband; only, this doctor took her money. Each time she called him he arrived, called the illness by a variety of long names that no one understood, not even himself, and each time charged her a fee. After two or three months, she got fed up with this carry-on and sent him running. She then sent for another doctor, then another, but each proved as useless as the last.

She eventually had to start selling off some of their fine cattle in order to raise money to pay for the doctors and their useless medicine. In the meantime, the farmer, who always had a great appetite before the illness and appeared to be well fed and stout of limb, now looked as though he was starving. He looked like a bag of bones; he didn't have an ounce of flesh on him and he could hardly walk. He had lost his appetite and whatever he did manage to eat was very little. He had great trouble swallowing; even when his wife soaked some bread in milk he found it hard to manage. Those who knew him said it looked as if he was a skeleton and it might be better for the poor man if he did die; at least he would be in no pain as he now appeared to be but a shadow of his former self.

One day, all the people of the house were out for the day, leaving the farmer alone. He was sitting outside, sunning himself, when a poor old man who was local to the area called by. The man was known by everyone and they were used to him asking for a bite to eat or a few coins. He spoke to the farmer, saying, 'Here I am again, asking for a few coins in the name of God. But, sweet mother of God, what's happened to you? You look terrible.'

The farmer replied, 'How are you, Seamus? It's good to see you. God knows what has happened to me for no one else seems to know, but I don't think I'm long for this world.'

'I'm sorry to hear that,' said the poor old beggar. 'When and how did this happen and what did the doctor say?'

'Doctors! Don't make me laugh, Seamus. I curse each and every one of the useless eejits. They know nothing except how to take money from you. I know, I shouldn't be cursing this near to the grave but at this stage I can't be bothered.'

'Maybe I could help? I have a little knowledge about herbs and things. If you were to tell me what ails you, I might be able to do something for you' said Seamus.

The farmer managed to smile and said, 'God bless you, Seamus, but I've seen the best doctors in the county. I've had to sell some of my best cattle to pay them and I never got an ounce of relief from any one of them. But I suppose it would do no harm to tell you how this happened to me.'

The farmer told the old beggar Seamus the whole story and what the doctors had said. Seamus listened carefully and when the farmer had finished his story he asked him, 'What kind of a field did you fall asleep in?'

'It was the meadow near the house. It was just after we had been gathering hay.'

'Was the grass wet at the time?' asked Seamus.

'No, in fact it was a lovely dry day. In fact, it was so warm that was why I fell asleep.'

'Was there a little stream or brook running through it?' asked Seamus.

'Yes, there was,' replied the farmer.

'Can I see this field?' asked Seamus.

'You can, of course. Come on, if you help me to stand up, I'll show you the way,' replied the farmer.

As sick as he was, he still managed by leaning on Seamus to walk to the field. Seamus examined the area where the farmer had lain down to sleep that fateful evening. He looked through the grass and weeds growing there, stooping down for a closer look. Eventually he stood up and said, 'It's as I thought.' Bending down once more, he picked up a little green herb and showed it to the farmer. 'Do you see this? Any place in Ireland you find this herb growing you will find an *Alp Luachra* nearby. It is the *Alp Luachra* that you are suffering from,' said Seamus.

'What on God's green earth is an *Alp Luachra* and how do you know that? If I swallowed something, surely the doctors would have found it?' replied the farmer.

'Ha, that pack of *amadáns* (fools). Sure, they know nothing of the old ways. Amn't I telling you, it was an *Alp Luachra* that you swallowed and if you want to get well, you'd better start believing me. Didn't you say yourself that you felt something moving around inside your stomach the first day you were sick? Well, that was the *Alp Luachra*; they jump around at first because they don't know where they are. The reason why you're so thin is because everything you eat the *Alp Luachra* is taking all the good out of it. Do you see the swelling on your side? Well, that's where he is living now,' said Seamus.

Of course, the farmer just laughed at him but the more he talked the more the farmer began to believe. When his wife and daughter returned home that day, Seamus told them everything he had told the farmer and strangely they believed him straight away. The farmer still had a few doubts but at last he agreed to call in a few of the doctors he had previously seen and told them his story.

The doctors gathered together but, having listened to both the farmer and Seamus, they burst out laughing and said, if there were any fools in the house it was the two of them and not the doctors. They insisted there was some medical reason for the farmer's illness; they came out with a few long words that no one seemed to understand (not even the doctors). Once again, they left him a few bottles of medicine, told the farmer's wife that she was just as big an eejit as the other two for believing such rubbish, charged her a fee and left the house still laughing at her.

'You know there's not a doctor in Ireland that'll do you any good. I suggest we go to see McDermott, the Prince of Coolavin, on the banks of Lough Gara. He's the best doctor in Connacht. In fact, I'd even say the best doctor in the five provinces,' said Seamus.

'Where is Lough Gara?' asked the farmer.

'It's in County Sligo. It's a big lake and the prince lives on the side of it. Take my advice and go there straight away for it's your last hope.'

Turning to the farmer's wife, Seamus said, 'If you want him to live, you must insist he goes.'

'I will of course. I'd do anything to make him live,' she replied.

The farmer said, 'Seamus, I'm willing to go anywhere and see anyone who may be able to help me, for if I don't get help soon I won't be long in this world.'

The following morning they set off for Lough Gara, all except the farmer's wife, who had to remain at home to look after the farm. Seamus and the daughter made a straw bed for the farmer in the back of a cart and harnessed the horse. They packed enough provisions to see them through the journey and set off for Sligo. They travelled slowly as the farmer was so weak the shaking of the cart upon the dirt roads was only just bearable but they found a welcome along the way in the isolated farmhouses they came upon.

Eventually, sometime on the third day, they arrived at Lough Gara and found the house of the prince in the early afternoon. It was a nice thatched cottage set in woodland and they went through the open door. Seeing someone who they found out was a servant, they asked if they could see the prince. The servant said he was eating a meal and he might come when he was finished, but just as he said that the prince entered the room and asked what was going on.

The farmer, who had sat down, now stood up and told the prince his story. He finished by asking, 'Can your honour help me?'

'I hope I can. Anyhow, I'll do the best I can as you have travelled far to see me. What Seamus has told you is true. You have swallowed an *Alp Luachra* or something just like it. Follow me,' replied the prince.

He led them to another room where there was a table upon which there were the remains of the meal he had been eating. Upon a large platter, there was a big piece of salted meat. He cut off a large slice, put it on a plate and gave it to the farmer to eat.

'I'm sorry, your honour, but I can't eat that. I couldn't even swallow a piece of meat the size of a wren's egg, never mind something the size of that.'

'Silence, man, and do as I tell you.' He then stood over the farmer and forced him to eat as much as he could. In fact, he made him eat so much, the poor old farmer thought he would burst. When the prince saw he really couldn't eat another mouthful he took him outside. He asked the farmer's daughter and Seamus to follow and led them down through a little meadow to the side of a stream and told the farmer to lie down with his face over the running water and his mouth open as wide as possible.

'Keep your face near to the water and stay like that, nice and quiet. If you value your life, don't move or make a sound until you see what happens to you.'

The farmer promised to do as he was told and he stretched out over the grass and held his mouth open over the gently running stream. The prince ordered everyone to move back a few metres, stand still and keep very quiet until he gave them permission to move. After about fifteen minutes, the farmer felt something moving inside him. He felt it slowly crawling up his throat and then running back down again. This went on three or four times until at last the thing, whatever it was, came as far as his open mouth. It stood on the tip of his tongue. Something caused it to panic – the sound of a bird, the movement of a small fish, who knows – but for some reason it ran back down his throat again. Within a minute or so, it reappeared. This happened two or three times but at last it stood upon the tip of the farmer's tongue once again. It smelt the water and leapt down into the little stream.

However, it didn't end there. The farmer felt another movement inside his throat, then another and another. The prince said, 'It would appear the thirst is on them; the salt in the meat seems to be working.' A second, third, fourth and fifth fell into the stream. However, the farmer continued to feel a movement inside his stomach. Eventually twelve of them had jumped into the stream, 'That's a dozen, but the old mother hasn't emerged yet.'

The farmer began to move, but the prince softly called out to him. 'Stay still. The mother hasn't come out yet.'

The farmer remained where he was. Time passed but there was no sign of the old mother *Alp Luachra*. The farmer was so tired, so weak, he attempted to rise but the prince and Seamus rushed forward and held his legs down so he couldn't get up. It seemed to take hours but eventually the poor farmer felt movement within his stomach, only this time it was far, far worse than anything he had felt before. He had to stop himself from screaming out in pain. Then it began to make its way up his throat. Just like before, it came out to the tip of his tongue and then shot back into his throat again. At last the farmer could stand it no longer and tried to grab it between his fingers but, quick as he was, the old *Alp Luachra* was quicker and it disappeared back down into his stomach.

'Arragh, you thick eejit! Didn't I tell you not to move? Stay still and she might come up again.'

Well, the poor old farmer stayed still for the best part of an hour because the *Alp Luachra* was now frightened and she had no intention of coming out. However, the thirst got the better of her and she eventually came back up the farmer's throat once more. She waited, looking out of his mouth until she was sure there was nothing to fear and then she jumped onto the tip of his tongue and plopped down into the stream to join her children. As soon as they saw her leave the farmer's mouth and land in the stream, the prince, Seamus and the farmer's daughter rushed over and lifted the farmer to his feet. He had been lying on the grass for hours. He was tired, sore and incredibly thirsty, but eventually he said, 'I feel like a new man.'

The prince insisted that they remained as his guests until the farmer felt well enough to make the return journey back to his farm. He refused any payment, insisting that it was payment enough for him to know that his cure had turned out so well. He also said that he felt they had paid enough over the past few months to various medicine men and doctors. The farmer, his daughter and Seamus arrived back home to a tearful welcome from the farmer's wife.

The farmer became healthy and just a little bit fat and felt marvellous. He was so thankful to Seamus for all that he had done and for his belief in him even when he had doubted himself that he insisted that he remain in the house as part of the family and Seamus lived there happily until his death years later. As for the farmer, well, he never lay down on the grass again – oh and if he ever felt any sickness or ill health, he never called upon the doctors he used to call on before and is it any wonder?

37

THE FROG

(*Losgann*)

FROGS ARE QUITE RECENT additions to the fauna of the Irish hedgerow and their exact method of introduction is unknown. Some suggest they were brought over by the Anglo-Normans. Yet others believe they were introduced sometime during the late 1500s or early 1600s by students of Trinity College Dublin, who had brought them here from England. They released the frogs into ponds and ditches that were around Trinity at that time; from there, they spread to all parts of Ireland and the rest is history. However, the frog is harmless and well thought of and appears to have found its niche in the rich habitat of the hedgerow.

Water is considered sacred to Druids and all water has its guardian spirits or deity. Frogs and their close relatives, toads, may be found in ditches at the edge of hedgerows or where riverine hedges grow. They spawn in water and will return to the place of their birth in order to carry out the cycle of life and for this reason they were thought to be representatives of the water spirits. Some even believed that a frog was the earthly manifestation of water spirits that lived in sacred wells and they were looked upon as a messenger of the water god/goddess who brought blessings of rain and purification.

Frogs were seen as creatures of the underworld and for this reason they became associated with witches and the supernatural, to be used in the preparation of potions and spells. Frogs were also believed to be one of the witch's familiars and that they would give warning to its mistress by loud croaking.

The frog, through its connection to Mother Earth, was considered lucky if it was living in the dairy for it protected the milk. But it was considered bad luck if a frog came into your house. However, never kill a frog that enters the house or camp or you stir death. It was once believed that a frog held the soul of a child who had died in childhood, especially if they had died in water, and for this reason if you kill a frog it will bring terrible misfortune.

The ancient Romans thought house frogs were lucky and kept live frogs as mascots. Many cultures consider it a sign that money is coming to you if a frog enters the house.

Finding a frog outside is lucky too, and if frogs live in your garden, good fortune will come to the house and all its occupants. In many Celtic countries, frogs are considered lucky and there are often stone frogs kept in the garden. Frog figurines have traditionally been given as house-warming gifts for this reason.

If you look at the colour of a frog, you can predict the weather: dark-coloured frogs are a sign of rain while light brown or yellow means that dry weather is on the way. There may be some truth in this as rain does make frogs darker and good dry sunny weather makes their skin a lighter colour, so who knows? A frog that croaks in the middle of the day is a sign that rain is due.

If you put a live frog in your mouth, it will cure toothache. (You had to rub the frog on the tooth or chew its leg.) The ashes of a cremated frog were thought to stop bleeding, its spawn was considered to be a cure for rheumatism and inflammatory diseases, and it was believed that if you rubbed a frog over a wart the wart would disappear. Sore eyes could be cured by getting someone to lick the eye of a frog and then lick the eye of the affected sufferer.

You can cure a cold by holding a frog by its legs and placing it in the sufferer's mouth for a moment (they'll be too busy vomiting to cough). If a child had whooping cough, it could be cured by bringing it to running water, putting a frog into the child's mouth three times and then letting the frog swim away uninjured. It would take the whooping cough with it. Is this where the saying 'I've got a frog in my throat' came from?

To create a love charm, bury a live frog in a box and after a few days dig it up. Take the skeleton apart and select a particular bone, place the bone in the clothing of the intended and they will fall madly in love with you.

Why Do the English Call the French 'Frogs'?

The main reason is that three frogs have been depicted on the heraldic device of Paris since ancient times – probably dating back to when Paris was a swamp. In pre-revolutionary France the common people of France were called *grenouilles*, or frogs, and the same name was later extended to include all the French people (by the English). Although some people will still believe it's because they eat frog's legs.

38

THE BLACKBIRD

(*Lon Dubh*)

BLACKBIRDS SYMBOLISE REINCARNATION AND are linked to the element of water. Place blackbird feathers under someone's pillow and they will tell you their innermost secrets.

Two blackbirds seen together mean good luck. The sight of two together is unusual as they are quite territorial. If they nest near your house, you will be lucky throughout the year and will experience good fortune. They are also regarded as messengers of the dead.

Blackbirds make their nests in trees from moss, grass and hair. A European tradition says that if human hair is used, the unfortunate unknowing donor will continue to suffer from headaches and possibly even boils and skin complaints until the nest is destroyed, so old hair should be disposed of carefully.

The beautiful song of the blackbird makes it a symbol of temptations, especially sexual ones. The devil once took on the shape of a blackbird and flew into St Benedict's face, thereby causing him to be troubled by an intense desire for a beautiful girl he had once seen. In order to save himself, the saint tore off his clothes and jumped into a thorn bush. This painful act is said to have freed him from sexual temptations for the rest of his life. Now if you believe that, you'll believe anything.

Like the crow and the raven, the blackbird is often considered a bad omen. Dreaming of a blackbird may be a sign of misfortune for you in the coming weeks. It also means you lack motivation and that you are not utilising your full potential. However, dreaming of a flying blackbird is said to bring good fortune.

One story concerning the blackbird is about St Kevin, an Irish seventh-century saint who loved wildlife. It is said that in the temple of the rock at Glendalough, St Kevin was praying with his hand outstretched upwards when a blackbird flew down and laid her eggs in his palm. The story goes on to say that the saint remained still for as long as it took for the eggs to hatch and the brood to fly the nest.

Among the Celts, the blackbird was thought to be one of the three oldest animals in the world, the other two being the trout and the stag. They were said to represent the water, air and earth.

Legend holds that the birds of Rhiannon are three blackbirds, which sit and sing in the World Tree of the Otherworld. Their singing puts the listener into a sleep or trance that enables her/him to go to the Otherworld. It was said to impart mystic secrets.

The whistle of the blackbird at dawn warned of rain and mist for the coming day and this may be where the following belief comes from. It was said that in Ireland in the nineteenth century, blackbirds held the souls of those in purgatory until Judgement Day and that whenever the birds' voices were particularly shrill, it was those souls, parched and burning, calling for rain. The rain always followed.

THE DUNNOCK

(Bráthair an Dreoilín)

ALSO KNOWN AS THE 'Irish Nightingale', the dunnock is surrounded by superstition. During day it is a happy little bird that tries to outdo every other bird with its song. However, at night its sad and tender songs are said to be the cries of unbaptised babies that have returned from the spirit world in search of their parents.

The dunnock's blue-green eggs were regarded as charms against witches' spells when strung out along the kitchen hob. They were especially good for keeping witches and spirits from coming down the chimney.

It was in fact Carl Linnaeus, the eighteenth-century Swedish-born botanist who gave the dunnock the name 'accentor', which means 'one who sings with another'. This family of birds are hedge-dwelling birds that are seen hopping around in a crouched position as they search for food. Chaucer noted that the cuckoo uses the dunnock to rear its young. Cuckoos that use dunnocks in this way can imitate the colour of the dunnock eggs, whereas other cuckoos which use another species of bird, say a meadow pipit, will imitate the colour of the meadow pipit eggs. Chaucer refers to the dunnock as *'hege-sugge'*, which means 'flutterer in the hedges'. *Hegesugge* is the Old English name for dunnock/hedge sparrow.

THE THRUSH

(Smólach)

THERE ARE MANY SUPERSTITIONS associated with song thrushes, including the notion that they dispose of their old legs and acquire new ones when they are about ten years old. Another superstition is that they are believed to be deaf. All sorts of things have also been said and written about mistle thrushes. In the fourth century, Plato was writing about its fondness for mistletoe and there is an old belief that mistle thrushes could speak seven languages!

In Ireland it was believed that the fairies made sure that the thrush built its nest low down, near the fairies home in the grass, so that they could enjoy the bird's song. If the thrush built its nest high up in a thorn bush, it was a sure sign that the fairies were unhappy and misfortune would come to the neighbourhood.

It was believed that the flesh of the song thrush would cure sickness and convulsions.

41

THE ROBIN

(Spideóg)

IF YOU HARM A robin's nest, you will be struck by lightning and if you break a robin's eggs expect something important of yours to be broken very soon. It is said to be extremely unlucky to kill this bird – the old saying goes, 'Kill a robin or a wren, never prosper, boy or man'. Some say that the hand that does so will continue to shake thereafter and traditionally the Irish believe that a large lump will appear on your right hand if you kill one. It is said that whatever you do to a robin, you will suffer the same tragedy. Some believe that cats will not even chase a robin.

A robin entering the house or tapping on a window foretells of a death to come. If a robin stays close to the house in autumn, a harsh winter can be expected. Robins are thought to be helpful to humans, occasionally granting favours. Robins are a sure sign of spring and if you make a wish on the first robin of spring before it flies off, you'll have luck throughout the following year.

When we think of a bird at Christmas, we usually think either of the turkey or the goose. However, the real bird of Christmas is the robin. He is found on Christmas cards, cake decorations and Christmas tree ornaments and is now recognised as a symbol of Christmas. The tradition was invented by the Victorians; when the first postal service was established in the 1840s, postmen wore a red uniform and they quickly became known as 'Robin Redbreasts'. In those days there were postal deliveries even on Christmas Day and so the robin and the postman became associated with the delivery of gifts.

There are several stories as to how the robin acquired its red breast feathers. In the Christian tradition, it is thought that a robin tried to remove the thorns from Jesus' head during the crucifixion and that drops of his blood fell onto the bird, staining his breast feathers red forever. In another myth, the robin gained his red breast from flying into the fiery wastes of hell to carry water to the stricken sinners who were suffering there for all eternity.

If you see a robin singing in the open, good weather is on its way, but if a robin is seen sheltering among the branches of a tree it will soon rain. A robin singing indicated a coming storm, while in the south-east of Ireland they believed that if a robin entered a house it was a sign of snow or frost.

If the first bird that you see on St Valentine's Day is a robin, it means that you are destined to marry a sailor!

Robins were believed to provide a cure for depression. The remedy suggests a robin must be killed and its heart removed. The heart should then be stitched into a sachet and worn around the neck on a cord.

It was widely believed that if a robin came across a dead body it would carefully cover the body with leaves and vegetation until it was completely hidden. This was depicted in *Babes in the Wood*, when the little bird buried the children, who had died of cold, with leaves. The ballad 'Who Killed Cock Robin' was first published in 1744 and Drayton in 1604 referred to the robin in his work entitled 'The Owlet'. In fact, there are many writers who have been inspired by the dear old robin.

How Robin Got his Red Breast

I've mentioned a couple of stories about how the robin got its red breast according to the Christian tradition. However, there are other tales about how the robin acquired his red breast feathers, so here are a couple of those.

One winter, a long time ago, Jack Frost was very cruel. He made the snow fall thickly upon the ground and he put ice on the ponds and frost on the windowpanes. The birds found it very hard to get food and soon they began to get hungry. Then, one day, the birds were sitting in a ring under a hedge, trying to think what was to be done. After a while a little brown, bird, called Robin, got up to speak.

'I have an idea,' he said. 'I will go into the gardens and try to get people to give us a lot more crumbs!'

Now Robin had a way all of his own of making friends. He went along to the houses where people lived and in one of the gardens he saw a man clearing away the snow from a path, so he hopped up very close to the man. Most birds are very much afraid of men, but Robin was brave. He had to be, if he was to help the other birds. When the man saw how friendly Robin was, and how hungry he seemed to be, he went into his house and fetched a tray full of crumbs. Robin was glad, and he flew off to fetch the other birds, and soon there were crowds of them in the kind man's garden. The best way they could say 'thank you' to the kind man was to eat the crumbs out of his hand. Robin then flew away into other gardens, and wherever he went he made friends. So, while the snow stayed on the ground the birds were able to feed after all.

At last Jack Frost sent the snow away and then the happy birds wanted to thank Robin so they made him a little red waist-coat, which he still wears. That is why he is now called Robin Redbreast.

OR

Many years ago, late in the year, a cruel wind brought biting cold weather, making the night more difficult for a father and son, who had travelled far and yet still had farther to go. They looked for a cottage, a barn, or even a tree, anywhere they might find shelter. However, there was nothing to be seen or found, except for a bush, and at last the father built a fire and told his son to try to sleep a little. When the father's eyes began to droop, he woke his son and told him to watch the fire. Well, how the boy tried to stay awake! He hadn't really slept while lying on the frozen ground and he was still exhausted from the walk. His eyes got lower. His head got lower. The fire got lower, so low in fact that a starving wolf began to inch nearer the sleeping pair. However, there was one who was awake; there was one who saw everything from the middle of an old bush – a little bird who was as gray as the brambly wood.

The bird hopped down and began fanning the flickering embers until the flames began to lick out hungrily; nor did the little bird stop, despite the pain in his breast, until the flames were dancing with strength. The heat from the flames changed the colour of his breast feathers and from that day onwards the robin has proudly worn a red breast.

THE WREN

(*Dreoilín*)

THE WREN IS A mouse-like little bird, scurrying here and there, hiding in ivy leaves and picking up insects in all sorts of hideaway places. Wrens were traditionally associated with the Druids of Ireland, who consider the wren a sacred bird and use their musical notes for divination. They were called '*magus avium*' (the magic bird) or *Dreoilín*, as derived from '*dreán*' or '*draoi éan*', the translation of which is 'druid bird'.

Irish tradition holds that the wren symbolises the old year, while the robin symbolises the year to come. To ensure that the passage from old year to new could take place, it was once common practice on St Stephen's Day (26 December) for a group of local boys to hunt and kill a wren.

This band of so-called Wren Boys, usually costumed and often masked, would then travel from house to house carrying the wren in a small box or casket (other sources say the wren was tied to a pole and decked with ribbons). They regaled each house with musical laments for the unfortunate bird, along with pleas to raise money for the funeral. One of the songs that they sang was as follows:

> The wren, the wren, the king of all birds
> On St Stephen's Day was caught in the furze,
> His body is little but his family is great
> So rise up landlady and give us a treat.

> If your treat be of the best,
> Your soul in heaven can find its rest.
> If your treat be of the small,
> It won't please the boys at all.

> A glass of whiskey and a bottle of beer,
> Merry Christmas and a Happy New Year,
> So up with the kettle and down with the pan
> Give us a penny to bury the wren.

This ancient tradition is still carried out in certain towns and villages in Ireland and it really is a sight to behold! The Wren Boys march through the streets dressed in traditional attire (usually something made from straw) to the beat of drums and they stop off in bars along the way to play traditional music. Money is still collected but this is usually given to charity and of course a wren is no longer killed. However, some Wren Boys still march carrying a fake bird.

Although the Wren Boys are rarely seen today, a historical thread links them to Ireland's past. Some sources say the wren is vilified because it had betrayed Irish soldiers who were staging an attack on the invading Norsemen. The Normans had been responsible for the destruction of some of the great monastic communities of early Christendom, such as the abbey at Kells. It is said that while pecking at some breadcrumbs left upon a drum, the wren alerted the Norsemen, betraying the hiding place of the Irish and leading to their defeat.

A similar story is told about the troops of Oliver Cromwell. When the Irish forces were about to catch Cromwell's troops by surprise, a wren perched on one of the soldier's drums. Making a noise, the wren woke the sleeping sentries just in time, thereby saving the camp and leading to the defeat of the Irish.

Other myths hold that the wren betrayed St Stephen with its chirping, leading to the first martyrdom of a Christian saint. Although the custom of sacrificing a wren is most commonly associated with Ireland, some form of the tradition actually exists throughout the Celtic world. Similar rites are found in the Isle of Man, Wales and France.

Other stories say that the hostility shown towards this most harmless of creature's results from the efforts of clerics in the Middle Ages to undermine vestiges of Druidic reverence and practices involving the bird.

The feathers of the wren were thought to prevent a person from drowning and because of this the feathers were traditionally very popular with sailors.

A traditional French belief holds that children should not touch the nest of a wren or the child will suffer from pimples. In the same way as a robin is revered, if anyone harms the bird then the person will suffer the same fate.

The Breton Druids have given the wren an honoured role in their folklore. They believe that it was the wren that brought fire from the gods but as she flew back down to earth her wings began to burn so she passed her gift to the robin, whose chest plumage began to burst into flames. The lark came to the rescue, finally bringing the gift of fire to the world.

The wren's eggs are said to be protected by lightning. Whoever tries to steal wren's eggs or even baby wrens would find their house struck by lightning and their hands would shrivel up.

The male bird builds two or three ball-shaped nests for the female to inspect. She decides which one she likes best and will then proceed to line the chosen nest, reading it for egg-laying.

Most Irish small birds become vegetarians for the winter, but the wren survives by persisting with a high-energy diet. However, the wren is so small it can suffer from loss of body heat in the winter. To help combat this, they become troglodytes (cave dwellers), burrowing into places with good insulation. Sometimes they will use their domed nests – very few bird species sleep in their nests, using them only for breeding, but wrens are an exception. They will also crawl into cracks in old trees, spaces behind facia boards, holes in stone walls or even in your barn.

Most of the year, wrens are fiercely territorial but they will abandon this trait in cold weather and will often roost together for extra warmth. There may be up to a dozen birds huddled into a tight ball; however, some communal roosts have been discovered with up to a hundred wrens in them. Remember: an odd nest box left up occasionally during the winter months will often be used for roosting. It is not unusual for several wrens to cuddle up together in one box during cold times.

How the Wren Became the King of All Birds

Once upon a time, somewhere in the west of Ireland, there was a secret valley. It was full of trees and close to the sea. Among the animals of Ireland it was known as the Valley of the Birds because it was there that all the birds of Ireland would meet at certain times of the year to discuss matters of importance and to sort out any problems they may have had.

At one of these meetings, the trees were covered with birds of all kinds. There were little birds like the robin red breast and the tiny wren, there were medium-sized birds like the chicken and the crow and there were big birds like the seagull and the golden eagle, with his sharp claws and fierce eyes.

The golden eagle said, 'I have been watching the humans and I saw that they have a king. I think we should have our own king.'

However, which bird should it be and how should they choose a king? The birds discussed the matter all day and late into the night.

The robin said, 'I should be king for the robin did a great favour for the Queen of the Fairies and as a reward she gave us this fine red waistcoat to wear so all other birds could see how brave and loyal the robin is.'

'Excuse me,' said the wren in a tiny little voice that none of the other birds could hear because of all the twittering and screeching that was going on.

The crow said, 'Caw'm off it, I should be king of the birds for the crow has followed the human and knows their ways. I also have the most beautiful black feathers, caw caw.'

'Excuse me,' said the wren.

The chicken said, 'Bu-bu-bu-but I should be king for I lay eggs that the humans have for breakfast. I live on their farms so I also know their ways and I have the most beautiful feathers of many different colours. Everyone loves me, so I should be king.'

'Excuse me,' said the wren.

The seagull said, 'I guide the human when they go to sea; I show them where they can catch fish and warn them of bad weather. They trust me. I should be king.'

'Excuse me,' said the wren,

The golden eagle said, 'I am bigger and fiercer than any of you. I can see further and am stronger and braver, I can fly higher, so I am your rightful king, you must choose me.'

'Excuse me,' said the wren.

The owl sat a little way off in the branches of a tree. He said nothing but all the birds knew he was the wisest of all birds.

'Let us ask the owl to choose our king,' cried the birds.

The owl agreed and chose two swans to help him decide and to act as referees. They also made the rules and made sure all the other birds in the competition obeyed them. No pushing, no scratching; that sort of thing.

The owl then said, 'We have decided that as we are creatures of the air the bird that flies the highest should be our king.'

The wren said in a tiny little voice, 'Yes, yes, the bird that flies the highest should be king.'

The owl looked at the wren, put his head to one side and said, 'Hoot, hoot.'

The wren thought to himself, 'The owl thinks he is the wisest of all birds but I'm wiser than he is and I already know which bird will fly highest.'

The owl said, 'Now the rules are simple, whoever flies the highest will be crowned king of all the birds in Ireland. Are there any questions?'

The eagle stretched out his wings, looked at the owl and said, 'Just one: where's my crown?'

'What do you mean?' squawked the magpie. 'We haven't had the competition yet. How do you know you are going to win?'

'Of course I'll win,' said the eagle. 'I am the best bird in all of Ireland.'

'Well, there is more to being king than being big and strong. To be a good ruler, you should be wise, kind and sensitive to others,' said the magpie.

'Shut yer face,' said the eagle. 'I'm going to win so there.'

The owl turned to all the other birds and said, 'Everyone ready? Flap your wings. Ready, steady, GO!'

They all took off in a cloud of feathers. They flew high above the earth, but one by one they grew tired and had to come back down to their homes. The owl and the swans watched and each thought they knew who would win, but they said nothing. The golden eagle beat his powerful wings and rose higher and higher. After a while he looked back and saw all the other birds far below him.

'This is easy. They'll never catch me. I'm going to win this easily,' he thought. Very pleased with himself, he went higher and higher until he could go no further. 'I've won! I'm the true king of all the birds in Ireland.'

He began to get ready to glide back down to earth. Just then, he felt something moving in the feathers on his back and he heard a tiny little voice say, 'Excuse me and thank you.'

The golden eagle looked over his shoulder and can you guess what he saw? Yes, it was the tiny little wren. The wren jumped off his back, up into the air and flapped his wings. He flew high above the eagle. The eagle was angry and tried to flap his wings again but by now he was too tired.

'Come back, come back! That's not fair! I'm the king of the birds,' screeched the eagle.

But the wren flew higher and higher. The eagle glided back down to earth and screeched in an angry voice, 'That's not fair. Tell the wren that he has cheated and it is not allowed.'

The wise old owl listened to the eagle, smiled and looked up to the tiny spot high above in the sky. The wren was coming back down to earth. The owl whispered to the two swans.

'Well?' demanded the eagle.

'We have made our decision,' said the owl to all the birds. 'Being a king means not only being big and strong and powerful. It also means being clever, thinking ahead and planning. The wren did not cheat; he simply outwitted you. For this reason we have decided that the wren will be king of all birds'.

That is the story of how the tiny wren became the king of all birds and he has been the king of all birds in Ireland ever since. As for the eagle, well, he decided he wanted nothing more to do with things and went to live on a mountain top and that is where eagles live to this day.

Cliona the Seductress

One of the most interesting legends is that of Clíona. She was a woman of the Otherworld who seduced young men to follow her to the seashore. Here they were drowned in the ocean into which she enticed them. Eventually a charm was discovered that not only protected against her wiles but could also bring about her destruction. Her only method of escape was to turn herself into a wren. As punishment for her crimes, she was forced to take the shape of the little bird on every succeeding Christmas Day and fated to die by human hands. Hence the barbaric practice of hunting the wren.

43

THE GOLDCREST

(Cíorbhuí)

THE GOLDCREST IS THE smallest bird in Ireland. Goldcrests are very difficult to see and yet are extremely common in the Irish countryside. The bird gets its name from its bright gold crest, which is very striking. The adult bird is about the size of an average human thumb and very light. They have a very distinctive high-pitched call, which sounds a bit like 'cheep, cheep'. One of the reasons they can prove difficult to spot is their extremely good camouflage; if you are lucky enough to spot them, it will usually be when they are foraging under hedgerows as they search for insects under fallen leaves. The male and female birds are almost identical.

The wren is erroneously assumed by many to be the smallest bird and there are many stories told of how the wren became the king of the birds. However, it is the goldcrest which is not only the smallest of all our birds but it also has the golden crown. In fact, the family of birds it belongs to is called 'Kinglets'.

The story of how the wren became king of all the birds in Ireland can be found in the chapter on the wren. However, the alternative ending of the tale, when applied to the goldcrest goes like this:

As the eagle soared high above all the other birds he proclaimed himself to be king.

'Well, here I am the highest of all,' called the eagle.

'Oh no, you're not,' answered the goldcrest, as, jumping from the eagle's back, he flew upward, until suddenly he knocked his head against the sun and set fire to his crest, which gave it the appearance of a crown. Stunned by the shock, the little goldcrest fell to the ground, but he soon recovered and he immediately flew up on to the royal rock and showed the golden crown that he now had upon his head. Unanimously he was proclaimed king of the birds and he has been known as the king of all the birds in Ireland ever since. His fiery crest is worn as proof of both his cunning and bravery.

44

THE MAGPIE

(*Snag Breac*)

THE MAGPIE IS NOT a native Irish bird. In fact, there was an absence of magpies in Ireland until they were first recorded by Solomon Richards, a colonel in Cromwell's army. He lived in Wexford town in 1682 and wrote about a strong easterly wind that brought with it a flock of magpies that he suggested came from either England or Wales. He commented on the fact that these birds had never been seen in Ireland before this. They landed in the Barony of Forth, where they remained and began to breed. Richards went on to say that magpies were a frequent visitor to his garden but they were spread more thinly in the rest of Ireland.

It has been suggested that the magpies having entered Ireland in the same county that the English first entered was an indicator of English invasion. Richards wrote, 'The natural Irish much detest them saying they shall "never be rid of the English while these magpies remain".' Hundreds of years later it was still said in certain parts of Ireland that 'As long as there are magpies left in this country, Ireland will never be at peace'.

The Kilkenny and South East Ireland Archaeological Society Journal of 1858–59 quotes an account written in 1684 by Robert Leigh of Rosegarland, Wellingtownbridge, County Wexford: 'About eight years ago there landed in these parts a new sort of planter out of Wales, a parcel of Magpies, forced I suppose by stormy weather, which now breed in several places in the Barony of Forth, and at a place called Baldinstowne in the Barony of Bargy.'

The bad press that surrounds the magpie is still prevalent today. In the farming community magpies are seen as a threat to livestock, especially sheep and new-born lambs, and this is in many ways founded on fact. Magpies and Crows have been witnessed by members of the farming community attacking young sheep and lambs. They have also been known to pick open fresh wounds on young animals, kill poultry and eat bird's eggs. However, man has, of course, done far more to eradicate various forms of wildlife and livestock than the carrion birds have ever done.

Folklore surrounding the magpie is extensive and the famous rhyme about the magpie ('One for sorrow, two for joy …'), which originated in England, has differing Irish and Scottish versions. The magpie is still thought to be a harbinger of the devil and if you see a single bird then it is believed to be a sign that bad luck will surely follow. However, there are many rituals to counteract this. You can salute or raise your hat to the bird and say, 'Good morning Mr Magpie, how's the wife?' the implication being that you hoped to see a second bird as the rhyme says 'Two for joy'. You may wave, or spit (although spitting is very unhygienic and shouldn't be done), and some people will make the sign of the cross. In County Mayo you put your hand in your pocket and held onto your money, just in case the magpie would steal it (we're awful cute in Mayo). The magpie was so hated in rural areas that between the years 1982 and 1984 almost 14,000 birds were culled by gun club members in County Cork alone and magpie control is still practised throughout Ireland up to this day.

The magpie is an intelligent bird and can be taught to imitate human speech, often learning to say a few words. It has a love of bright objects, which it will steal if given a chance.

It was believed that if a magpie landed on the roof of your house it was a sure sign that the house would not fall down or suffer badly in a storm. It has been suggested that this belief springs from the story that the magpie wouldn't go into the ark but spent the whole time sat on the roof during the heavy rain. However, there is another belief that if you see a magpie on your roof then it means that someone inside is sure to die, especially if the magpie is chattering.

In Ireland a group of magpies is known as a parliament, no one is sure why. I like to think it's because when they join together they tend to be full of useless chatter and they never really seem to do anything.

The magpie is considered one of the sacred birds of the Druids and this may account for its bad press during the times of the early Christian Church. There is an old folktale that states that when Jesus was crucified on the cross, all the world's birds wept and sang to comfort him in his agony. The only exception was the magpie, and it is for this reason that the magpie is forever cursed. Another tale, along a similar line, states that the magpie carries a drop of Satan's blood under his tongue. This was his reward for not wearing a full mourning suit at the crucifixion.

The magpie is known for its lifelong pairing and loyalty to its mate and it is believed that when a magpie's mate dies it summons an assembly of other magpies at which the dead bird is honoured before a new mate is selected. The old rhyme, for those who haven't heard it before, goes like this:

One for sorrow,
Two for joy,
Three for a girl,
Four for a boy,
Five for silver,
Six for gold,
Seven for a secret never to be told,
Eight for a wish,
Nine for a kiss,
Ten a surprise you should be careful not to miss,
Eleven for health,
Twelve for wealth,
Thirteen beware it's the devil himself.

The Magpie's Nest

Here are a couple of stories about the magpie and its nest-building:

Once upon a time, the magpie started to build a nest but it wasn't going well so all the other birds decided to give her a bit of advice. However, each piece of advice was met with the response, 'Arragh I knew that before you said it'. Eventually the patience of all the other birds was exhausted and they left her to finish building her nest on her own, the result being that to this day the magpie's nest seems to remain unfinished.

However, as with a lot of stories in folklore, there is another version:

All the birds of the air came to the magpie and asked her to teach them how to build nests, for the magpie is the cleverest bird of all at building nests. So she put all the birds round her and began to show them how to do it. First of all she took some mud and made a sort of round cake with it.

'Oh, that's how it's done,' said the thrush and away it flew away, and so that's how thrushes build their nests.

Then the magpie took some twigs and arranged them round in the mud.

'Now I know all about it,' said the blackbird, and off he flew and that's how the blackbirds make their nests to this very day.

Then the magpie put another layer of mud over the twigs.

'Oh, that's quite obvious,' said the wise owl, and away it flew and owls have never made better nests since.

After this the magpie took some twigs and twined them round the outside.

'The very thing!' said the sparrow, and off he went; so sparrows make rather untidy nests to this day.

Well, then the magpie took some feathers and bits of sheep's wool and lined the nest very comfortably with it.

'That suits me,' cried the starling and off it flew; and starlings have had very comfortable nests ever since.

So it went on, every bird taking away some knowledge of how to build nests, but none of them waiting to the end. Meanwhile the magpie went on working and working without looking up until the only bird that remained was the turtle dove and that hadn't paid any attention all along, but only kept on saying its silly cry: 'Take two, Taffy, take two-o-o-o.'

At last the magpie heard this just as she was putting a twig across. So she said, 'One's enough.'

But the turtle-dove kept on saying, 'Take two, Taffy, take two-o-o-o.'

The magpie got a little angry and said, 'I said one's enough.'

But the turtle dove cried, 'Take two, Taffy, take two-o-o-o.'

At last, having finished, the magpie looked up and saw nobody near her but the silly turtle-dove and then she got really angry and flew away and refused to tell the birds how to build nests again.

And that is why all the birds build their nests differently.

45

THE OWL

(*Scréachóg Reilige*)

THE BARN OWL IS known for its long, eerie shriek and it is for this reason that it has also become known as the screech owl. This bird has a reputation for being the wisest of birds and yet it has also developed a bad reputation that stems from the fact that it is a solitary bird that leads a nocturnal existence. It has been suggested that this is why it has been associated with the darker forces that are said to walk the earth in the hours of night. It has even been said that to see one during the day is a sign of bad luck.

The barn owl is now on the Red List as a threatened species due to many factors, such as loss of habitat, road accidents and changes in agricultural practices. They mate for life so the loss of a mate is devastating.

Should an owl brush its wings against a window pane or be seen perching for a considerable length of time on a roof then it is traditionally believed that illness and even death is present within. One superstition says an owl that enters the house must be killed at once, for if it flies away it will take the luck of the house with it.

To look into an owl's nest is reputed to leave the observer with a sad and morose soul.

According to an old tradition, if you hear an owl hooting in a densely built-up area then a female in the locality has just lost her virginity!

A dead owl has served many purposes. One is to ease the pain of gout by mixing some of the flesh with boar's grease to create an ointment. Owl broth was once feed children to prevent them contracting whooping cough and it was also believed to turn grey hair back to its original colour. Any man who eats roasted owl will be obedient and a slave to his wife.

The eggs were once thought to help prevent epilepsy, bad sight (for obvious reasons) and to bring drunks back to their senses.

Due to the barn owl's eerie appearance, its habit of screeching and nesting in old abandoned buildings and churches, people believed it was associated with ghosts and death. Many people used to believe that owls swooped down to eat the souls of the dying. If they heard an owl hooting, they would become frightened. A common remedy was to turn your pockets inside out and you would be safe. An alternative, more extreme, solution was to take off your clothes, turn them inside out and put them back on. You might not want to do this if you are in public.

To counter evil owl power, put irons in your fire or throw salt, hot peppers or vinegar into the fire. The owl will get a sore tongue, hoot no more, and no one close to you will be in trouble.

Witches were thought to transform into owls and suck the blood of babies. It was believed that you could discover a person's secrets by placing a feather or part of an owl on him while he was sleeping.

The custom of nailing an owl to a barn door to ward off evil and lightning persisted into the nineteenth century.

Carrying an owl's foot and heart was once believed to protect its bearer from contracting rabies if they were bitten by an infected dog.

The Wise Old Owl

Once upon a time long, long ago, a large group of owls came to settle in a wood. The wood was full of lovely green trees and they were each allowed to pick a tree of their choice in which to build their nests.

Each of the young owls chose a green, luscious, and healthy tree for themselves but there was an old owl in the group and the younger owls forced him to live in an old, half-dead tree. The old owl had to be satisfied with his tree and settled down for the day. As time went by, the younger owls, who felt proud of their trees, would tease the old owl and would shout at him, saying, 'Hey, old man, what's the matter? Couldn't you find a nice tree? Your tree is half dead and dry-looking, a bit like yourself,' and they all laughed at him.

The old owl would silently smile; he was very wise. At times he would reply to their insults, saying, 'Who knows whether you are lucky to live in your tree or if I am lucky to live in mine?' However, the young owls would just laugh at him and fly away.

One day a group of woodcutters came into the wood in search of timber. The tall green luscious trees were perfect for them and they took out their sharp axes and started to chop them down. The young owls started making loud noises when they saw their homes being destroyed but they couldn't do anything about it. They had to sit helplessly and watch the destruction. Eventually the woodcutters came to the old and half-dead tree. They said, 'No

point in wasting energy cutting this old thing down. It's of no use
to us.' So they left it where it stood and went on their way. The old
owl's nest was spared.

So you see, what you think is a curse can sometimes be a blessing
in disguise.

Wise as an Owl

Once upon a time, a long time ago, when the world and all the
animals were being made, the owl was in a queue, waiting to talk
to God. God had already given the owl a voice, two eyes, a head, a
body and strong wings but he wanted to ask God to give him a long
neck like the swan, jet-black feathers like the crow and a powerful
beak like the eagle.

Now God was extremely busy trying to do all those things that
God does but he patiently listened to the owl. He agreed to give
the owl everything he asked for but he would have to wait his turn.

Now God had a few rules and one of those rules said that no
one was allowed to watch him work and he looked at the owl and
said, 'Your eyes are open and you know that you are not allowed
to watch me when I'm working. Go away; keep your eyes shut and
wait until I call you. I'm busy creating a rabbit.' With that, God
turned to the rabbit, the rabbit was shaking and looking rather
nervous. Well, you know what rabbits are like. God asked him,
'What would you like, little rabbit?'

'I'd like long legs and ears,' the rabbit said quietly. 'Oh and can I
have fangs and sharp claws please? I'd really like sharp claws.'

God snapped his fingers and the rabbit's ears and long legs
appeared. God then sat and stroked the rabbit's ears, smiled and said,
'I think I could manage a nice set of fangs and some sharp claws.'

The owl who was standing nearby hooted loudly and said,
'Stupid creature, why don't you ask for something useful, like
wisdom? What are you going to do with fangs and claws?'

God got rather annoyed and turning towards the owl he said, 'I've already warned you: stop looking at me when I'm working. Mind your own business, be quiet and wait your turn.'

The owl, full of his own importance, turned to God and with an angry glare said to him, 'Now you listen to me, God, you have to give us what we ask for and I demand you give me wisdom.'

'You were warned but you would not listen,' sighed God.

He slapped the top of the owl's head down into his body, which made his neck disappear, and shook the owl so much that the owl's eyes opened wide in fright. Then he pulled both the owl's ears until they stuck out from his body. God then said to him, 'I've made your ears big so you might listen when you are told something; I have made your eyes bigger so you might see where you're going wrong; and I've given you a short neck so you may hold your head still. Your head is now packed with wisdom, as you demanded, so I advise you to fly away before I take back what I have given.'

The owl was no longer a fool and he took God's advice and flew away as fast as his wings would take him, hooting and screeching as he went.

God smiled and turned back to the rabbit but by this time the rabbit had run off; he didn't like arguments and shouting. So he never did get his fangs and sharp claws, but maybe someday.

As for the owl, well, he knew he had angered God and he also realised that if he was ever to anger him again then he would lose all that he had gained. Because of this, the owl will only come out at night, when he thinks that God is asleep.

46

THE RAVEN

(An Fiach Dubh)

THE RAVEN, WITH ITS glistening purple-black plumage, large size and apparent intelligence, has inspired man from ancient times and is interchangeable with the crow in Irish folklore. Ravens are associated with knowledge, warning, procreation, healing, and prophecy and are also a form favoured by shape-shifters. They are considered to be one of the oldest and wisest of animals. 'To have a raven's knowledge' is an Irish proverb meaning to have a seer's supernatural powers to see all, to know all and to hear all. Giving a child their first drink from the skull of a raven will give the child powers of prophecy and wisdom.

Ravens were considered royal birds. Legend has it King Arthur turned into one and they were the favourite birds of the solar deity, Lugh, who was said to have had two ravens that attended to all his needs.

The raven and crow were regarded as omens of both good fortune and bad, carrying the medicine of magic. They are often associated with war, death and departed spirits. Ravens flying towards each other were seen as an omen of war and a raven was said to have alighted on the shoulder of the Ulster hero, Cúchulainn, to symbolise the passing of his spirit.

In Irish folklore the raven and the crow were associated with the Triple Goddess, the Morrigan. It was believed that the raven/crow that flew over the battlefield was the Morrigan. Some would consider her the protector; others looked upon her as the bringer of death. She was, however, the protector of warriors. Her message really should be that in war there can only be one winner and that is death.

The raven is believed to be an oracular bird and a bearer of messages from the Otherworld. It is a symbol of the connection between this world and the next and it was said to represent the balance between life and death and the creation of the new. As a symbol of death, the raven would be buried with its wings outstretched in order to symbolise the connection between this world and the Otherworld and the raven as a messenger between the two.

When crows were quiet and subdued during their midsummer's moult, some European peasants believed that it was because they were preparing to go to the Devil to pay tribute with their black feathers.

Banshees could take the shape of ravens or crows as they cried above a roof, an omen of death in the household below. A single crow over a house also meant bad news, and often foretold a death within: 'A crow on the thatch, soon death lifts the latch.' Other omens of death within a household included seeing a raven tapping on a window, hearing a raven croaking near the house or seeing a raven flying around the chimney. It has been said that a baby will die if a raven's eggs are stolen.

However, the raven has not always been associated with death, spirits and darkness. Quite the contrary, the raven was believed by some to be the bringer of light, truth and goodness. The Bible (Genesis 8: 6-13) tells how birds are sent by Noah to detect whether there is any dry land outside the ark that he had built to withstand the Flood: 'At the end of forty days Noah opened the window of the ark which he had made, and sent forth a raven; and it went to and fro until the waters were dried up from the earth.'

Many parts of Celtic Britain and Ireland view the raven as a good omen. In Wales, if a raven perches on a roof, it means prosperity for the family and in Scotland deerstalkers believed it bode well to hear a raven before setting out on a hunt. In Ireland ravens with white feathers were believed to be a good omen, especially if they had white on the wings. Ravens flying on your right-hand side or croaking simultaneously were also considered good omens.

Finding a dead crow on the road is good luck but crows in a churchyard symbolise bad luck. Crows feeding in village streets or close to nests in the morning means inclement weather is to come – usually storms or rain. Crows flying far from their nest means fair weather. Ravens facing the direction of a clouded sun foretell hot weather and if you see a raven preening, rain is on the way.

The raven is said to be the protector and teacher of seers and clairvoyants. The Druids would predict the future by studying the flight and the cries of the birds. In Shetland and Orkney, if a maiden sees a raven at Imbolc she can foretell the direction of her future husband's home by following the raven's path of flight.

Two crows would be released together during a wedding celebration. If the two flew away together, the couple could look forward to a long life together. If the pair separated, the couple might expect to be soon parted. (This practice was also performed using pairs of doves.)

The Romans used the expression 'To pierce a crow's eye' in relation to something that was almost impossible to do. An Irish expression, 'You'll follow the crows for it', meant that a person would miss something after it was gone.

The expression 'I have a crow to pick with you' was used a lot in the mid/southern states of America and was a way of describing an issue to be argued over (a bone of contention). The similar expression 'I have a bone to pick with you' has been in use since as early as the sixteenth century. Both expressions may have resulted from witnessing two dogs or two crows arguing and pulling at the last piece of meat on a bone.

In the past, witches were thought to turn themselves into ravens to escape pursuit and they could also be used to create a spell for invisibility. Cut a raven's heart into three, place beans inside each portion, and then bury them right away. When the bean sprouts, keep one and place it into the mouth. Invisibility occurs while the bean is inside the mouth.

The Vanity of the Crow

Once upon a time, long, long ago, the creator of the world said that he or she intended to appoint a king over all the birds. A day was named when all the birds should send a representative to appear before the creator and on that day one of them would be selected. The one selected to rule as king would be the most beautiful of them all.

As they all wanted to look their best, the birds began to wash, dust, and generally preen their feathers for the big day. The crow was there along with all the rest and realised that with his ugly plumage he stood no chance of being chosen, so he waited until they were all gone and then he picked up the most colourful feathers the other birds had dropped and fastened them onto his own body. Now he looked better than any of them.

When the day arrived to appear before the creator, all the birds assembled before the throne. After walking up and down and looking at each bird, the creator decided that the crow was the most beautiful and should be crowned king of all the birds. All the other birds were annoyed so they began to pull off the false feathers from the crow and eventually exposed him for the fraud he was.

So remember: it's not only fine feathers that make fine birds.

47

THE GOLDFINCH

(*Lasair Choille*)

GOLDFINCHES HAVE THE FOLK name 'thistle-tweaker'; this may be due to their love for the seeds of thistles and teasels which they prise out with their beaks. You can, if you wish, purchase identical seeds from garden centres or pet supply shops but the goldfinch will probably ignore them as they seem to have developed an insatiable appetite for peanuts. However, their love for sharp seeds and thorns, which they use for lining their nest, have given them a place in folklore.

A medieval legend tells that when Christ was carrying the cross to Calvary a goldfinch came down and plucked a thorn from the crown around his head. Some of Christ's blood splashed onto the bird as it drew the thorn out, and to this day goldfinches have spots of red on their plumage (a similar story is told about the robin). Renaissance artists frequently depicted the Christ child with a goldfinch, and it is suggested that the bird is linked to a foretelling by Christ of the manner of his death – something often attributed to the great folk heroes.

There is a Valentine's Day tradition based around birds. If the first bird a girl sees on that day is a blue tit, she will live in poverty; a blackbird foretells marrying a clergyman; a robin tells of a sailor; and if she sees a woodpecker she will be left an old maid. If the first bird she sees is a goldfinch, however, she is promised a wealthy marriage.

Here in Ireland there is a tradition that goldfinches, under their other name of redcaps, are said to haunt the realms of the fairy folk and they will always be seen around the *raths* or *sidhes* (fairy forts and mounds), and in hawthorn trees.

Their modern name comes from the old English *goldfinc*. The stripe of yellow on the wing is apparent even when the birds are flying. A group of goldfinches is called a charm; this derives from the Middle English *charme* and the Latin *carmen*, meaning a magic song or spell, and may be related to the sound they make when gathered together.

Goldfinches, along with most other finches, tend to be more social outside the breeding season. Flocks of goldfinches roost together in the inner branches of trees, particularly oak and beech trees. Some roosts can contain hundreds of birds but generally they are smaller. Goldfinches often join with greenfinches, chaffinches and linnets to form communal roosts. The roost site can change from one night to the next, but they can use the same one for prolonged periods. Their roosts can be several miles away from where they feed so they have to do a lot of travelling. They leave early in the morning to feed and then usually have a rest during the day so they will find a suitable roost site in daylight as well.

48

THE BLUE TIT

(*Meantán Gorm*)

EXTREMELY COMMON IN IRELAND, the blue tit is the typical hedgerow or woodland bird and has adapted well to living in close proximity to humans. Blue tits have been given many names throughout history, including tom tit, blue bonnet and tit mouse; in fact, they were known for a long time as tit mice. The name tit mouse is said to have derived from an old English word *titmouse*, meaning small bird. It has also been suggested that the name has Norse origins and the first use of titmouse has been dated to the fourteenth century.

The male and the female are almost identical, although the male is slightly brighter in colour. They are the only members of the tit species with a blue colouration. Their bright yellow breast feathers are maintained by eating caterpillars that are rich in carotene; the more they eat the brighter the colour. Females will choose mates that have the brightest yellow feathers. I suppose this may be an indication of the male's prowess as a good hunter and for this reason he will prove to be a good provider. The blue crown feathers are said to glow in ultra-violet light and it has been suggested that blue tits see the world in ultra-violet light.

Blue tits nest in holes in trees and walls but will use manmade objects as well. In Ireland they have been seen nesting in postboxes, traffic lights and they have even taken advantage of our smoking ban as they have been seen nesting in wall-mounted ashtrays outside premises. Around the end of April, the female blue tit will lay one egg per day for up to twelve days – this coincides with the vast numbers of the caterpillar they are particularly fond of. The eggs will hatch in about fourteen days and then the parents' work really begins.

They will make around 400 trips a day backwards and forwards to the nest in order to feed the chicks; this will increase to around 1,000 trips per day just prior to the young leaving the nest. The parents will collect caterpillars from the leaves of trees (usually oak), eating only the small caterpillars themselves. The biggest and juiciest ones will be left in the nest to supply the chicks with the energy they will need to begin their new life. The ability of the blue tit to collect caterpillars makes them extremely effective as pest controllers in the garden. Blue tits have only one brood a year and if food is scarce or the weather turns against them many of the chicks will die. They are short-lived birds and may only have one chance to give birth and when the chicks leave the nest it will only be about three weeks old; it will be looked after for a further two weeks but then it's on its own and will have to fend for itself.

The blue tit has adapted well to living in close proximity to humans and will take any opportunity to make use of food supplies in our gardens. It has become a common and welcome sight around the feeders and bird tables of Ireland. In the city areas the blue tit has been known to remove the tops of milk bottles and drink the cream from the top of the milk. It has been said that the birds lack the enzyme necessary to digest lactose; in fact drinking milk causes them to suffer from diarrhoea. However, the cream of the milk contains no lactose so it is both safe and full of energy. An extremely intelligent bird, they have solved complex obstacles and puzzles and solved numerous problems in order to get to peanuts in feeders.

The blue tit does not fly far from its home and it is for this reason that they are seen as good omens for sailors. When sighted, it is a sure indication that you are not far from land. Blue tits are also believed to carry the souls of sailors who have died at sea to their eternal resting place in heaven. Because they were seen as 'soul carriers', if you killed a blue tit then it would result in great misfortune.

POSTSCRIPT

FOR THOSE OF YOU who have accompanied me upon this journey along the hedgerow, I thank you. I hope that it has awakened in you a love of all the beauty of the nature that surrounds us. The Irish hedgerow is linear woodland and as such it is one of our most important assets. It must be nurtured, managed and held in trust for future generations, both human and non-human. We need to become participants in nature rather than separating ourselves from it. By doing so we will develop a sense of belonging to the land and the flora and fauna that we all depend upon. If, by reading this book, you have developed an understanding of the importance of the hedgerow as an ecosystem, a treasure chest of folklore, an aid to mental well-being and its role in biodiversity, then I am content. I hope that you continue your journey, as you rediscover all that our beautiful landscape has to offer you and future generations to come.

In memory of Tony Locke